❧

BURN BRIGHT, NOT OUT

The Playful Guide To Recharging

ALICIA ANN WADE

Burn Bright, Not Out

COPYRIGHT © 2023 THE GRATITUDE METHOD TM

All rights reserved. No part of this book may be used or reproduced in any form whatsoever without written permission except in the case of brief quotations in critical articles or reviews.

This book is a work of fiction. Names, characters, businesses, organizations, places, events and incidents either are the product of the author's imagination or are used fictitiously. Any resemblance to actual persons, living or dead, events, or locales is entirely coincidental.

DISCLAIMER

Because of the dynamic nature of the Internet, any web addresses or links contained in this book may have changed since publication and may no longer be valid. The views expressed in this work are solely those of the author and do not necessarily reflect the views of the publisher, and the publisher hereby disclaims any responsibility for them. The author of this book does not dispense medical advice or prescribe the use of any technique as a form of treatment for physical, emotional, or medical problems without the advice of a physician, either directly or indirectly. The intent of the author is only to offer information of a general nature to help you in your quest for emotional and spiritual well-being. In the event you use any of the information in this book for yourself, which is your constitutional right, the author and the publisher assume no responsibility for your actions.

For more information, or to book an event, contact :

info@thegratitudemethod.com

http://wwwthegratitudemethod.com

Printed by The Gratitude Method TM

Printed in the Australia
ilable from Website and other retail outlets

ting Edition, 2023
5459228-0-6

Dedication

To all my CEOs, Leaders, Coaches, Speakers and Influencers of the world. Remember your light shines brightly, and to always remember not to burn out. This goes out to you and your souls!

Table of Contents

Introduction

    Understanding Burnout: Causes and Symptoms

    Importance of Addressing Burnout

Chapter 1
The Journey of Self-Discovery

    Recognizing Your Personal Triggers

    Exploring Your Values and Goals

Chapter 2
Daily Journaling for Reflection and Healing

    Establishing a Journaling Routine

    Prompts for Self-Reflection and Emotional Release

Chapter 3
The Power of Self-Care

    Defining Self-Care and Its Benefits

    Creating a Personalized Self-Care Plan

    Weekly Self-Care Rituals

Chapter 4
Embracing Mindfulness and Self-Compassion

    Practicing Mindfulness in Daily Life

    Cultivating Self-Compassion and Letting Go of Perfectionism

Chapter 5
Building Resilience Through Self-Love

    Nurturing Self-Love and Positive Self-Talk

    Strategies to Boost Self-Esteem

Chapter 6
Making Meaningful Experiences

    Finding Joy in Small Moments

    Pursuing Passion Projects and Hobbies

Chapter 7
Redefining Success and Setting Boundaries

    Rethinking Success: Quality vs. Quantity

    Setting Healthy Boundaries to Prevent Burnout

Chapter 8
Gratitude Practice and Prayer

    Cultivating Gratitude for Well-Being

    Incorporating Gratitude into Daily Life

    Exploring the Role of Prayer and Spiritual Connection

Chapter 9
Creating Supportive Relationships

    Building a Support Network

    Communicating Your Needs and Seeking Help

Chapter 10
The Role of Physical Health

    Exercise, Nutrition, and Sleep

    Holistic Approaches to Well-Being

Chapter 11
Sustaining Change and Preventing Relapse

    Monitoring Progress and Adjusting Strategies

    Strategies for Long-Term Burnout Prevention

Conclusion

    Celebrating Your Journey

Embracing a Balanced and Fulfilling Life

About the Author

Books By The Author

INTRODUCTION

Finding Light Beyond Burnout

In a world that often glorifies hustle and achievement, it's all too easy to find ourselves trapped in the unrelenting grip of burnout. I know this journey all too well, as it mirrors a personal story that once had me caught in its suffocating embrace. My name is Alicia Wade, and I invite you to embark on a transformative journey through the pages of this book – a journey that promises to guide you out of the shadows of burnout and into the radiant light of a balanced, purposeful life.

Not too long ago, in the year 2015, I found myself navigating life on a treadmill that was spinning at a dizzying pace. As an Operations Manager, I was entrusted with the monumental responsibility of not only managing state-regional meetings but also shouldering the load of tasks usually reserved for a second-in-command state manager. I found myself saying "yes" to every task that came my way, often working an exhausting 14 to 16 hours a day, all while juggling the challenges of being a full-time parent to a young child.

It was a life defined by survival, not thriving. The weight of demanding responsibilities at work, coupled with the strain of a difficult home environment, took its toll on my well-being. The stress of compliance, coupled with an all-consuming fear of letting others down, blurred the lines between passion and the dangerous tendency to be a chronic people-pleaser.

Happy times seemed distant, and the idea of taking a break was a foreign concept. Even during moments of illness, I'd find myself chained to my laptop, striving to fulfill expectations despite a clear need for self-care. A turning point came when my laptop finally succumbed to the pressure, a literal explosion of stress-induced burnout. It was then that I realized the urgent need for change.

In 2019 and 2020, as the world of coaching beckoned, I found myself wearing multiple hats – a national trainer, a development coach, an area manager, a director, and a student. Regarded as a powerhouse by some, I was slowly crumbling under the weight of the all-or-nothing mindset. My health paid the price, leading to two kidney infections due to neglecting my body's needs.

By 2020, the seeds of burnout had firmly taken root once more. Struggling to balance entrepreneurship with financial uncertainty, I worked tirelessly to please everyone around me. The 16-hour workdays became my norm, and sleep took a backseat as I fought to stay afloat. My identity was shaped by external demands, and my daughter became a fleeting presence in my life.

Then, in 2021, the inevitable crash arrived. The light that once burned within me was extinguished. The relentless pursuit of external validation had left me feeling lost, unable to recognize the person I had become. Darkness surrounded me, and the desire to escape it all became overwhelming.

But from this place of darkness, a glimmer of hope emerged. Through introspection, support, and the power of transformational strategies, I rediscovered the path to reclaiming balance and purpose. This book is an invitation for you to join me on this journey – to learn from my experiences, to embrace strategies that can guide you out of burnout's clutches, and to find the light that resides within you.

As we navigate the chapters ahead, we'll delve into the transformative practices of self-care, self-compassion, gratitude, and more. Together, we'll unravel the complexities of burnout and embark on a journey toward a life that radiates with well-being, fulfillment, and the unwavering belief that you deserve nothing less.

The journey from burnout to balance is not only possible; it is your birthright. Let's begin.

Understanding Burnout: Causes and Symptoms

Burnout is more than just exhaustion; it's a complex and multifaceted phenomenon that affects every aspect of our lives. To effectively overcome burnout, we must first dive deep into the underlying causes and recognize the subtle yet telling symptoms that often go unnoticed in the chaos of our daily routines. In this chapter, we'll explore the anatomy of burnout, shedding light on its origins and unveiling the warning signs that demand our attention.

The Slow Descent: Unraveling the Causes of Burnout

As we trace the roots of burnout, my own journey offers a poignant reflection. In 2015, my own burnout was fueled by a potent cocktail of overwork, excessive people-pleasing, and the inability to say "no." My ambition, while admirable, pushed me to juggle more responsibilities than one person could reasonably handle. As an Operations Manager, I strived to meet the expectations of both my professional and personal life, losing sight of the boundaries required for a healthy equilibrium.

For many, similar triggers lie at the heart of burnout. The relentless pursuit of success, coupled with the fear of failure, can lead to a pattern of overexertion that erodes our physical, emotional, and mental well-being. External pressures to perform, conform, and meet unrealistic standards create a breeding ground for the burnout beast to take hold. The constant tug-of-war between personal aspirations and societal demands can wear down even the strongest of individuals.

Symptoms in Shadows: Unmasking the Signs of Burnout

The symptoms of burnout often lurk beneath the surface, easily dismissed as normal stress or fatigue. Yet, they are the body's cry for help, a plea to recalibrate before the damage becomes irreversible. My own journey into burnout was marked by sleepless nights, relentless headaches, and a general sense of numbness. The passion that once fueled my work was replaced by a hollow ache, and joy became a distant memory.

Recognizing these signs early on is paramount. The exhaustion that creeps in, making even the simplest tasks feel insurmountable, should never be ignored. Emotional detachment, cynicism, and a growing sense of ineffectiveness are further indicators that burnout has taken root. The harmony between work and personal life becomes disrupted, as the lines blur and permeate into one another. The incessant feeling of being trapped in a hamster wheel is a clear warning that burnout is knocking on our door.

By understanding the causes and symptoms of burnout, we begin the journey of reclaiming balance. This chapter serves as a foundation, guiding us toward an exploration of practical strategies that empower us to untangle ourselves from burnout's grasp. As we unravel the complexities of this phenomenon, we gain the insight needed to recognize burnout's presence and intervene with intention and care.

Let's continue this journey of understanding, for only by comprehending the roots of burnout can we hope to rise above it. In the chapters that follow, we'll explore actionable steps and transformative practices that can pave the way to renewed vitality, purpose, and well-being.

Importance of Addressing Burnout

In a world that celebrates productivity and achievement, the importance of addressing burnout cannot be overstated. It's not simply a matter of enduring a tough phase; burnout is a silent intruder that, left unchecked, can wreak havoc on our physical, emotional, and psychological well-being. As we navigate the fast-paced currents of modern life, understanding why confronting burnout head-on is vital becomes a cornerstone in the path towards holistic wellness and lasting success.

Unraveling the Web of Consequences

To truly grasp the urgency of addressing burnout, one must peel back the layers to uncover the domino effect it triggers. My own journey from thriving professional to burnout survivor highlighted this all too clearly. The relentless pursuit of success, driven by the desire to meet every demand and excel in every arena, saw me tangled in a web of escalating consequences.

The most immediate cost was my physical health. The sleepless nights, the skipped meals, and the consistent disregard for my body's needs ultimately led to exhaustion, weakened immunity, and even kidney infections. Mentally, the joy and passion I once held for my work dimmed to a flicker, replaced by a pervasive sense of disillusionment. Emotionally, I found myself irritable and detached, my relationships and personal life casualties of my relentless pursuit of perfection.

The effects of burnout ripple outwards, impacting not only our well-being but also our performance and contributions in all areas of life. In a professional context, burnout diminishes productivity, stifles creativity, and drains the passion that once fueled our pursuits. Personally, it strains relationships, erodes our ability to find joy in everyday moments, and leaves us feeling isolated even in a crowded room.

The Call to Reclaim Balance

Addressing burnout isn't a luxury; it's a necessity. It's a call to reclaim the balance that has been skewed by the pressures of modern life. It's a decision to prioritize well-being, not as an afterthought, but as a fundamental pillar upon which we build our lives. When we confront burnout head-on, we recognize that self-care isn't indulgence; it's a responsibility that allows us to show up fully for ourselves and for others.

When we acknowledge the importance of addressing burnout, we dismantle the notion that burnout is synonymous with success. True success isn't found in pushing ourselves to the brink; it's rooted in self-awareness, resilience, and the ability to maintain equilibrium even amidst life's challenges. By committing to address burnout, we rewrite the narrative, replacing the glorification of busyness with a celebration of well-being.

In the pages that follow, we'll embark on a journey of transformation, exploring practical strategies, insightful practices, and powerful mindset shifts that empower us to not only overcome burnout but to thrive in its aftermath. By addressing burnout, we're not only investing in our present but also shaping a future that's characterized by vitality, fulfillment, and a renewed sense of purpose.

Let us embrace the urgency of addressing burnout with open hearts and open minds, for the journey ahead promises not only healing but also the rediscovery of the vibrant, resilient individuals we are meant to be.

Burn Bright, Not Out

The Playful Guide To Recharging

Burn Bright, Not Out

Chapter 1
The Journey of Self-Discovery: Unveiling the Path to Renewal

In a world that constantly demands more from us, the journey of self-discovery shines as a guiding light through the fog of burnout. It's a journey that invites us to step away from the whirlwind of external pressures and venture inward, where we unearth the treasures of our true selves. As we navigate this chapter, we'll delve into the "why" behind embarking on this transformative expedition, the myriad benefits it offers, and the profound impact it has on reclaiming health and vitality in our lives.

The Deeper "Why"

In a society marked by hustle culture and ceaseless striving, the allure of the journey of self-discovery beckons with an irresistible promise: the promise of authenticity, alignment, and a profound sense of purpose. Burnout rates are alarmingly high, affecting individuals across industries and walks of life. According to a 2021 survey conducted by the American Psychological Association, a staggering 89% of respondents reported feeling overwhelmed by stress, and 62% cited work as a significant source of stress in their lives. The consequences of chronic stress and burnout extend far beyond the individual, reaching into workplaces, families, and communities.

Amid this unsettling reality, the journey of self-discovery stands as a beacon of hope, a way to disrupt the cycle of burnout by addressing its roots. Research has shown that individuals who engage in self-discovery practices experience higher levels of emotional well-being, reduced stress, and increased resilience. By embarking on this journey, we are taking a proactive step towards redefining our relationship with stress, forging a path toward lasting well-being.

The Rich Benefits of Self-Discovery

The benefits of embarking on a journey of self-discovery are as varied as they are transformative. By peeling back the layers of societal expectations, we tap into the wellspring of our true passions and values. This self-awareness becomes a compass guiding us toward making decisions aligned with our authentic selves, rather than choices dictated by external pressures. Research by the Center for Creative Leadership underscores the connection between self-awareness and leadership effectiveness, highlighting how understanding oneself leads to improved decision-making, communication, and overall performance.

In the quest to overcome burnout, the journey of self-discovery serves as a foundation upon which we can rebuild our lives. It allows us to set healthier boundaries, to say "yes" to opportunities that resonate with our values, and to confidently say "no" to commitments that drain our energy. As we uncover our strengths and areas for growth, we foster resilience that empowers us to navigate life's challenges with greater grace and determination.

The Role of Health and Vitality

The journey of self-discovery isn't merely a voyage of the mind; it's a quest for holistic well-being. Studies have shown that individuals who engage in practices that align with their values and passions experience reduced stress-related health problems, improved immune function, and increased life satisfaction. By acknowledging the interconnectedness of our physical, emotional, and psychological well-being, we forge a path toward health and vitality that extends far beyond the confines of burnout.

As we embark on this chapter's exploration of the journey of self-discovery, let us remember that this voyage isn't a luxury; it's a necessity. It's a step towards reclaiming our identities, cultivating resilience, and living lives marked by purpose and fulfillment. By undertaking this journey, we breathe life into the notion that we are more than our to-do lists and obligations – we are complex beings deserving of the time and space to discover, nurture, and celebrate our true selves.

Recognizing Your Personal Triggers: Unmasking the Catalysts of Burnout

Triggers – they're the subtle whispers that set off a cascade of emotions, thoughts, and reactions, often propelling us down a path towards burnout. Understanding these triggers is akin to holding the key to unlocking the doors to our well-being. In this section, we'll explore the essence of triggers, unveil the art of identifying them, and delve into the labyrinth of symptoms they incite. Most importantly, we'll arm ourselves with strategies to not only overcome these triggers but also pave the way for a future defined by enhanced wellness and well-being.

The Anatomy of a Trigger

A trigger is akin to an emotional tripwire, a stimulus that propels us into a heightened state of emotion or stress. It can be an external event, a comment, a situation, or even an internal thought pattern that ignites a series of reactions within us. These reactions aren't merely surface-level; they often trigger deeper emotional responses that have roots in past experiences, beliefs, and personal history.

Unveiling the Triggers: How to Identify Them

Identifying triggers requires a blend of self-awareness and curiosity. It involves a willingness to explore our emotional landscapes and trace patterns in our responses. Paying attention to situations or conversations that evoke intense emotions – whether that's anger, anxiety, or sadness – can often point us toward our triggers. It's not just the immediate emotional response that matters; it's also about uncovering the underlying beliefs and thought patterns that amplify the emotional reaction.

The Trail of Symptoms: Navigating Trigger Responses

Triggers are seldom solitary incidents; they usually set off a series of symptoms that can be both emotional and physical. Emotional responses may include heightened irritability, mood swings, or a sense of helplessness. Physically, triggers can manifest as increased heart rate, shallow breathing, or tension in the body. Recognizing these symptoms is a crucial step in the process of overcoming triggers, as it empowers us to intervene before they escalate into burnout-inducing territory.

Strategies for Overcoming Triggers

Overcoming triggers isn't about eliminating them entirely – it's about developing a toolkit of strategies that allow us to respond to them in healthier ways. Mindfulness practices, such as deep breathing or grounding exercises, can help us stay centered when faced with triggering situations. Cognitive reframing, where we challenge negative thought patterns associated with triggers, empowers us to regain a sense of control over our responses. Seeking support through therapy or coaching can also provide insights and techniques for managing triggers effectively.

Shaping a Future of Wellness and Well-Being

The process of recognizing and overcoming triggers isn't just a remedy for the present; it's an investment in a future marked by enhanced wellness and well-being. By acknowledging and addressing triggers, we dismantle the unconscious patterns that fuel burnout. We cultivate emotional resilience, empowering ourselves to navigate life's challenges with grace and self-compassion. As we liberate ourselves from the clutches of triggers, we pave the way for a life defined by authenticity, purpose, and a profound connection to our inner selves.

In the chapters that follow, we'll delve into practical exercises, empowering techniques, and insightful practices that guide us in the journey of recognizing, understanding, and ultimately overcoming triggers. By undertaking this exploration, we take an essential step towards building a foundation of well-being that extends far beyond the boundaries of burnout.

Exploring Your Values and Goals: Navigating the Compass of Purpose

Amid the chaos of modern life, where burnout threatens to engulf us, the journey to reclaim balance begins with a compass guided by our values and goals. This section invites us to embark on a profound exploration, delving into the core of our being to unearth the values that define us and the goals that propel us forward. Through a systematic process, we will navigate the labyrinth of self-discovery, weaving a tapestry of intention that leads us away from burnout and towards a life infused with purpose and fulfillment.

The Foundation of Values and Goals

Our values are the invisible threads that weave the fabric of our lives. They shape our decisions, influence our actions, and determine the choices we make. Goals, on the other hand, provide the roadmap for our journey, casting a guiding light on the path we choose to tread. By aligning our values with our goals, we forge a powerful synergy that propels us toward a life that resonates with authenticity and meaning.

The Process of Unveiling: A Systematic Approach

Unveiling our values and goals requires a systematic approach that encourages deep introspection. Begin by setting aside a quiet moment, free from distractions. Close your eyes and imagine your ideal life – one that's free from constraints, expectations, and judgment. What does this life look like? What values are evident in your daily experiences? What goals do you aspire to achieve? Note down any thoughts, feelings, or images that arise during this contemplation.

Next, list your values – the qualities that are non-negotiable in your life. These could range from integrity and compassion to creativity and adventure. Then, consider your goals – both short-term and long-term. What aspirations ignite your passion? Which dreams resonate with your values?

Activity: Your Values and Goals Declaration

To solidify this journey, let's engage in an empowering activity: creating your own Values and Goals Declaration. Set aside dedicated time and find a peaceful space. Craft a statement that captures the essence of your values – the guiding principles that define who you are. This could be as simple as "I value authenticity, compassion, and growth."

Next, articulate your goals with specificity and intention. These goals can span various facets of life – from career and relationships to health and personal development. Craft a concise yet meaningful sentence for each goal. For instance, "I aim to cultivate a supportive work-life balance that allows me to thrive both professionally and personally."

By weaving your values and goals into this declaration, you're not only affirming your commitment to a life aligned with purpose but also creating a tangible reminder that you can revisit whenever you need to realign with your authentic path.

A Future Guided by Purpose

Exploring your values and goals isn't a mere exercise in introspection; it's a deliberate act of self-definition that shapes the course of your life. By uncovering your values and setting clear goals, you equip yourself with an unerring compass that guides you away from burnout's treacherous waters. With this newfound sense of purpose, you're prepared to navigate the challenges of life with resilience, authenticity, and a renewed vigor.

In the chapters that follow, we'll venture deeper into the landscape of self-discovery, exploring practices that empower you to align your actions with your values and propel your journey towards the goals that resonate with your soul. Your declaration of values and goals serves as the cornerstone upon which you build a life that radiates with authenticity, intention, and an unwavering commitment to your well-being.

Exploring Your Values and Goals: Crafting Your Personal Blueprint

In the labyrinth of modern life, where burnout thrives, the journey of self-discovery embarks upon a crucial juncture – the exploration of your values and goals. This chapter unveils a roadmap, a step-by-step process, to navigate this terrain with clarity and purpose. Through deep introspection, journaling, and deliberate self-inquiry, you will unearth your core values, define your aspirations, and craft a personal blueprint that guides you away from burnout's grip and towards a life illuminated by intention and fulfillment.

Step 1: Create a Sacred Space

Find a quiet, comfortable space where you can sit uninterrupted. Have your journal and pen ready. Dim the lights, light a candle if it resonates with you, and take a few deep breaths to center yourself. This is your sacred cocoon for introspection.

Step 2: Reflect on Moments of Aliveness

Close your eyes and journey into your memory bank. Recall moments when you felt truly alive and aligned with yourself. Was it a personal achievement, a meaningful interaction, or a creative endeavor? Reflect on why these moments stood out to you. What values were at play? Was it adventure, connection, authenticity?

Step 3: Delve into Your Past

In your journal, create a timeline of your life. Mark significant milestones – achievements, challenges, turning points. For each milestone, jot down the emotions you felt and the underlying values that were present. For example, a promotion might evoke a sense of accomplishment, linked to your value of growth.

Step 4: Identify Your Core Values

From your reflections, list the recurring values that echo through your memories and experiences. These are your core values – the principles that resonate deeply with who you are. Prioritize these values by ranking them in order of importance. Challenge yourself to narrow it down to a meaningful few.

Step 5: Set SMART Goals

With your core values as the compass, it's time to set goals that reflect your aspirations. Utilize the SMART framework: Specific, Measurable, Achievable, Relevant, Time-bound. For instance, if a core value is health, a SMART goal could be: "I will exercise for 30 minutes, 3 times a week, to improve my physical well-being within the next 3 months."

Step 6: Visualize Your Ideal Life

Imagine your life a year from now, five years from now, a decade from now. Envision the life you desire, deeply aligned with your core values and guided by your goals. What do you see, feel, hear? How do your values and goals shape your interactions, choices, and daily routines?

Activity: Crafting Your Personal Blueprint

In your journal, dedicate a page to your Personal Blueprint. Start by listing your prioritized core values. Under each value, articulate the specific SMART goals that resonate with that value. Describe how achieving these goals aligns with your envisioned life. Remember, this is a living document that will evolve as you do.

A Future Forged with Intent

Crafting your Personal Blueprint isn't just a cerebral exercise; it's the act of defining your path with intention. By unearthing your values and setting aligned goals, you fashion a roadmap that safeguards you from burnout's clutches. This blueprint becomes your anchor, guiding you with clarity and purpose.

As we continue this journey, we'll delve deeper into practices and techniques that translate your values and goals into daily actions. This isn't just a chapter; it's a transformative compass, guiding you towards a life that's illuminated by authenticity, intention, and well-being. Your Personal Blueprint is your declaration to life – a declaration of self-honor and a commitment to a life well-lived.

Chapter 2
Daily Journaling for Reflection and Healing: Unveiling the Power Within

Amid the whirlwind of a world that often demands more than we can offer, the practice of daily journaling emerges as a sanctuary for self-reflection and healing. It's a voyage of introspection, an intentional pause amidst chaos, a whispered conversation with your own soul. In this chapter, we dive into the realm of daily journaling, unearthing why it's a vital component of reclaiming balance. Backed by research and the wisdom of centuries, we'll explore how this practice empowers you to navigate burnout's treacherous waters and chart a course towards renewal.

A Ritual of Vital Importance

In a society perpetually on the move, where burnout thrives as a silent epidemic, daily journaling becomes a sacred ritual of vital importance. Research conducted by Dr. James Pennebaker, a pioneer in the field of writing therapy, has shown that expressive writing – the act of putting your thoughts onto paper – has profound psychological and physiological benefits. Journaling allows us to externalize our internal struggles, gaining insight into our emotions, thoughts, and patterns.

The Healing Alchemy of Journaling

Each stroke of the pen carries the potential to heal wounds that often go unnoticed. The act of journaling isn't confined to mere writing; it's an act of self-compassion, a gesture of self-love. By expressing our innermost thoughts, we engage in a process that not only rewires our minds but also triggers a healing cascade through our mind, body, and spirit.

Unveiling the Unconscious: The Power of Self-Reflection

Daily journaling becomes a portal to self-awareness – a lantern that illuminates the corridors of our psyche. As we pour our thoughts onto paper, patterns emerge, revealing the triggers, habits, and beliefs that drive our actions. It's a journey towards the deeper layers of our unconscious mind, a dance between bringing consciousness to what once resided in the shadows.

Moving from Fight or Flight to Conscious Awareness

In a world often driven by the primal instincts of fight or flight, daily journaling shifts the narrative towards conscious awareness. It allows us to step out of reactionary mode and into a space of mindful response. By witnessing our thoughts and emotions on paper, we empower ourselves to choose our responses, fostering emotional intelligence and resilience.

The Journey Forward: Unleashing the Benefits

The benefits of daily journaling are as diverse as they are profound. It reduces stress, as proven by a study published in the Advances in Psychiatric Treatment. It enhances emotional regulation, boosting our capacity to navigate life's challenges with grace. It nurtures creativity, empowering us to tap into the wellspring of inspiration. Most importantly, it serves as a compass that guides us away from burnout's precipice and towards a life steeped in well-being.

Through the Lens of Reflection and Healing

As we dive deeper into the art of daily journaling, we'll explore practices, prompts, and techniques that empower you to harness this potent tool. This chapter isn't just about scribbling thoughts; it's about carving out time to engage in a sacred dialogue with yourself. By nurturing self-reflection and embracing the healing power of daily journaling, you cultivate a haven of well-being within. You unravel the threads of burnout, stitching together a tapestry of renewal and empowerment. The pages of your journal become a testament to your journey towards balance, one word at a time, one healing stroke of the pen. The look from the current theme or using a format that you specify directly.

Establishing a Journaling Routine: Nurturing Your Self-Care Sanctuary

In the landscape of our bustling lives, the practice of journaling becomes a sanctuary for self-care and healing. It's a space where thoughts unfurl, emotions find expression, and healing begins its gentle dance. To fully harness the transformative power of journaling, establishing a consistent routine is paramount. In this section, we'll explore the why, how, and steps of creating a journaling routine that not only serves as a form of self-care but also as a profound tool for healing.

Why a Consistent Routine Matters

Consistency is the heartbeat of change. Just as drops of water shape rock through their persistent rhythm, a daily journaling routine molds the contours of our well-being. A routine anchors the practice, making it a non-negotiable part of your day. Research suggests that forming habits rewires the brain, reinforcing positive behaviors and making them second nature. By weaving journaling into your daily routine, you're gifting yourself the time and space for introspection and healing.

Crafting Your Journaling Ritual: Step by Step

Designate a Time: Choose a time of day that aligns with your natural rhythms and schedule. It could be in the morning, a peaceful pause during lunch, or a reflective moment before bed.

Create an Inviting Space: Set the stage for your journaling ritual. Find a cozy corner, light a candle, play soothing music – anything that helps you transition into a reflective mindset.

Gather Your Tools: Prepare your journal, a pen you love writing with, and any other materials that enhance your experience. Make this process enjoyable, a form of self-care in itself.

Set a Ritual: Engage in a short pre-journaling ritual to signal the start of your practice. It could be taking a few deep breaths, stretching, or sipping a cup of herbal tea.

Choose Your Prompt: Decide on a prompt that resonates with you. It could be as simple as "Today, I feel..." or a more specific question related to your goals or emotions.

Write Freely: Let your thoughts flow without judgment. This isn't about perfection; it's about authenticity and self-expression.

Reflect and Close: After writing, take a moment to reflect on what you've penned. Close your journal with a sense of completion and gratitude.

Creating a Supportive Environment

Your journaling environment should be a haven that beckons you daily. If possible, designate a specific spot for this practice. Surround yourself with items that inspire tranquility – soft cushions, calming scents, or inspiring artwork. Make this space your refuge, a sanctuary where you can connect with yourself without distraction.

Infusing Routine with Ritual

Routine and ritual intertwine to create a practice that's both methodical and sacred. Rituals signal your brain that it's time to transition into a specific mindset. Incorporate simple rituals like lighting a candle, taking a few deep breaths, or setting an intention before you begin journaling. These rituals act as bridges between the ordinary and the sacred, transforming your practice into a form of self-care and healing.

The Journey Forward: A Ritual of Healing

By establishing a journaling routine, you gift yourself a profound act of self-care and healing. This routine is an oasis of reflection in the midst of chaos, a lifeline that anchors you amidst life's tides. As you weave journaling into your daily life, you not only engage in a transformative practice but also reframe your relationship with self-care. It becomes a non-negotiable, a ritual of healing that leads you towards burnout's exit and into the realm of balance and well-being.

Prompts for Self-Reflection and Emotional Release: Navigating the Depths of Your Soul

Within the pages of your journal lies a gateway to your inner world, a canvas upon which you can paint the tapestry of your emotions, thoughts, and aspirations. To fully harness this transformative practice, engaging in self-reflection and emotional release becomes an art. In this section, we'll explore the power of prompts that beckon you to dive deep and let go. We'll also guide you through a step-by-step process to release emotions in a healthy way, combining the healing currents of breathing and journaling.

The Path of Self-Reflection: Prompts that Illuminate

Gratitude Exploration: Reflect on what you're grateful for today. Dive into the small joys that often go unnoticed. This practice shifts your focus to the positive, fostering resilience and well-being.

Unearthing Core Values: What values guide your choices and actions? List them and reflect on how they show up in your daily life. This prompts alignment between your values and actions.

Challenging Beliefs: Identify a limiting belief you hold. Write about its origins and how it influences your choices. Challenge it with evidence that contradicts it.

Future Self Conversation: Write a letter to your future self – one year from now. Envision the changes you'd like to see and the progress you hope to make.

Dear Inner Child: Pen a letter to your inner child, acknowledging their experiences and offering reassurance and love. This practice nurtures emotional healing.

Emotional Release: A Step-by-Step Guide

Find a Calm Space: Begin by finding a quiet, comfortable space where you won't be disturbed. Sit or lie down in a relaxed position.

Focus on Your Breath: Close your eyes and bring your attention to your breath. Breathe in deeply through your nose, allowing your abdomen to rise. Exhale slowly through your mouth, releasing tension.

Tune into Your Emotions: As you continue to breathe deeply, tune into the emotions you're feeling. Notice where in your body you're experiencing them.

Express through Breath: With each inhale, imagine you're breathing in calm and healing energy. With each exhale, release the emotions that no longer serve you.

Journaling for Integration: After this breathing exercise, open your journal and write about the emotions you released. Reflect on any insights or shifts you experienced during the process.

A Dance of Healing and Liberation

Prompts for self-reflection and emotional release are invitations to a dance of healing and liberation. As you put pen to paper, you create a bridge between your conscious mind and the depths of your emotions. Journaling allows you to process your feelings, understand their origins, and gain perspective. By combining it with a breathing practice, you amplify the release, allowing stagnant energy to flow out of your body.

This union of breath and journaling isn't just an exercise; it's a portal to self-discovery, emotional well-being, and transformation. As you engage in this dance, you grant yourself permission to let go of what no longer serves you and create space for healing and growth. The pages of your journal become a canvas for your emotions, a container for your thoughts, and a pathway towards liberation.

Chapter 3
The Power of Self-Care: Nurturing the Well that Nourishes All

In the symphony of modern life, self-care stands as the conductor that orchestrates harmony between our outer endeavors and inner well-being. Yet, I once stood amidst the crescendo of hustle, caught in the relentless rhythm of meeting external demands and pleasing others. Not a day was dedicated to tending to my own well-being. It was as if I was a gardener nurturing every plant but my own.

It's a story that resonates with many – the tale of a life defined by obligations and commitments, while the whispers of self-care are buried beneath the clamor of the world. In this chapter, we illuminate the transformative power of self-care, uncovering the radiance it bestows upon our lives when we pause, embrace, and fill our own cup.

The Neglected Oasis Within

Imagine a garden where every flower is nurtured except one – a striking metaphor for a life that neglects self-care. Our bodies and minds, akin to that forgotten flower, wilt under the weight of unmet needs. Just as a garden flourishes when each plant receives nourishment, our lives thrive when self-care becomes the foundation upon which we build our days.

The Elixir of Restoration

The absence of self-care erodes our vitality, dims our resilience, and distances us from our own essence. In my own journey, when I paused to nurture my well-being, I witnessed an alchemical transformation. I was no longer depleted but filled with vigor. Self-care became the elixir that restored my soul, enabling me to not only weather life's storms but to dance through them.

A Quote to Live By

As we navigate the dance of self-care, a quote by Audre Lorde echoes as a guiding light: "Caring for myself is not self-indulgence, it is self-preservation, and that is an act of political warfare." In a world that romanticizes busyness and glorifies overextension, prioritizing self-care is a revolutionary act. It's a declaration that our well-being matters, that our cups must be filled before we pour into others.

Filling Your Cup: The Journey Forward

In the chapters that follow, we'll delve into practices, rituals, and strategies that transform self-care from an elusive concept into a steadfast commitment. We'll explore how to integrate self-care seamlessly into your daily life, creating a sanctuary where you replenish, renew, and flourish. Just as a river nourishes the land it flows through, let self-care be the river that nourishes your soul, sustaining you as you navigate the currents of life.

Defining Self-Care and Its Benefits: Cultivating a Lifeline of Well-Being

In the cacophony of modern existence, self-care emerges as a lifeline, offering a refuge of well-being amidst the chaos. It's not merely a fleeting indulgence; it's a deliberate act of nourishing your body, mind, and soul. In this chapter, we'll delve into the multifaceted nature of self-care – its purpose, essence, and the transformative benefits it bestows upon your life. Supported by research and wisdom that spans generations, we'll unveil why, what, and how self-care is a vital commitment to yourself.

The Why Behind Self-Care

Imagine a jug that pours into countless cups without ever being refilled – a metaphor for a life that's constantly giving, but seldom replenishing. The journey of self-care begins with understanding that your well-being is a non-negotiable cornerstone of your existence. Just as a well cannot yield water if it's empty, you cannot give from an empty vessel. Prioritizing self-care is an act of honoring your own worthiness and vitality.

The What of Self-Care

Self-care is more than bubble baths and spa days; it's a holistic commitment that touches every facet of your being. It's carving out time for activities that uplift your spirit, nurturing your body through movement and nourishment, and cultivating a mental landscape of compassion and balance. From journaling and meditation to leisurely walks and quality sleep, self-care encompasses actions that align with your well-being.

The How of Self-Care

Embracing self-care is a dance that begins with self-awareness. It's about tuning into your body, listening to your emotions, and recognizing your needs. It involves setting boundaries, saying no when necessary, and allowing yourself permission to pause and rejuvenate. Self-care isn't a luxury; it's a requirement for thriving in a world that demands so much.

The Transformative Benefits of Self-Care

1. Reduced Stress: Numerous studies, including one published in the Journal of Clinical Psychology, underscore the positive impact of self-care on reducing stress. Engaging in self-care practices activates the parasympathetic nervous system, promoting relaxation and counteracting the fight-or-flight response.

2. Enhanced Emotional Well-Being: Research conducted by the University of California, Berkeley, shows that self-care contributes to greater emotional resilience and improved mood regulation. Engaging in activities that bring joy and relaxation fosters emotional balance.

3. Improved Physical Health: The American Psychological Association emphasizes the connection between self-care and physical health. Regular exercise, balanced nutrition, and adequate sleep are all facets of self-care that support overall well-being.

4. Increased Productivity: Contrary to the belief that self-care is time-consuming, research from Stanford Graduate School of Business reveals that taking regular breaks and practicing self-care enhances productivity, creativity, and focus.

5. Strengthened Relationships: Self-care nourishes your relationship with yourself, which in turn improves relationships with others. When you prioritize your well-being, you're more emotionally available and able to cultivate healthier connections.

6. Empowerment and Resilience: A study published in the Journal of Individual Differences shows that self-care fosters a sense of empowerment and personal agency. Engaging in activities that align with your values and well-being builds resilience in the face of challenges.

The Call to Nurture: A Life Transformed

Self-care isn't a luxury reserved for special occasions; it's a foundation upon which you build a life marked by vitality and joy. By embracing self-care as an intentional commitment, you tap into the wellspring of well-being that resides within. As you embark on this chapter's exploration, remember the wise words of Audre Lorde: "Caring for myself is not self-indulgence, it is self-preservation." By prioritizing self-care, you embark on a transformative journey of self-preservation, empowerment, and a life that radiates with well-being.

Creating a Personalized Self-Care Plan: Crafting Your Compass of Well-Being

In the tapestry of modern life, self-care isn't a mere luxury; it's a navigational tool that guides us toward a life marked by vitality and balance. Just as a ship's captain charts a course, you too can embark on a journey of well-being by creating a personalized self-care plan. In this chapter, we'll unravel the steps, questions, and insights that empower you to craft a self-care compass – one that leads you away from burnout's treacherous waters and into the calm harbor of self-nurturing.

Step 1: Set Your Intention

Begin by asking yourself: What does self-care mean to you? What areas of your life need nourishment? Your intention acts as the guiding star, directing your self-care efforts toward what truly matters.

Step 2: Identify Your Needs

Reflect on your physical, emotional, mental, and spiritual needs. What practices or activities resonate with each aspect? Do you need movement, solitude, creative expression, or connection? List these needs to lay the foundation of your self-care plan.

Step 3: Assess Your Current Habits

Take stock of your current routines and habits. Which ones support your well-being, and which ones deplete you? What activities or behaviors could be replaced with self-care practices? This step uncovers areas where your self-care plan can be integrated seamlessly.

Step 4: Define Realistic Goals

Set achievable self-care goals that align with your needs. Use the SMART framework – Specific, Measurable, Achievable, Relevant, Time-bound. For instance, if you're aiming to improve sleep, a SMART goal could be: "I will create a calming bedtime routine and aim for 7-8 hours of sleep each night within the next month."

Step 5: Create a Weekly Schedule

Map out your week, allocating time for self-care activities. Consider both daily practices and longer activities that require planning. Aim for balance and flexibility, allowing yourself to adapt as life unfolds.

Step 6: Cultivate Mindfulness

Integrate mindfulness into your self-care plan. Before engaging in each practice, take a moment to center yourself. Be fully present, savoring the experience without distraction.

Step 7: Regular Self-Check

Set aside time each week to reflect on your self-care plan. Are you honoring your intentions and goals? Are there any adjustments needed? Regular self-checks ensure your plan remains dynamic and responsive to your evolving needs.

Questions to Guide Your Journey

What activities make me feel rejuvenated and joyful?

How can I incorporate self-care into my daily routine?

Are there any habits I need to release to make space for self-care?

What boundaries do I need to set to protect my well-being?

How can I make self-care a non-negotiable part of my life?

A Compass to Navigate Life

Creating a personalized self-care plan isn't just an exercise; it's a proclamation of self-worth and a commitment to nurturing your well-being. As you embark on this journey, keep the metaphor of a compass in mind. Your self-care plan acts as your compass, guiding you towards well-being in the same way that a navigational tool guides a ship through uncharted waters. By crafting a self-care plan tailored to your needs and intentions, you equip yourself with a powerful tool that supports your journey towards a life defined by balance, vitality, and inner harmony.

Weekly Self-Care Rituals: Nourishing Heart, Soul, and Well-Being

Amidst the whirlwind of life's demands, carving out time for self-care rituals becomes an act of self-love and a sanctuary for healing. This chapter unveils a treasure trove of 100 self-care rituals, carefully curated to nourish your heart, elevate your soul, and foster personal growth. From the simple to the profound, these rituals beckon you to infuse your week with intentional moments of well-being. To assist you in creating a harmonious routine, we've provided a Table of Contents for you to fill out, a guide to map your journey towards a life brimming with self-nurturing.

Table of Contents: Your Self-Care Ritual Journey

Week Starting :   /   /

Day 1:

Morning Ritual:

Description:

How it makes me feel:

Afternoon Ritual:

Description:

How it makes me feel:

Evening Ritual:

Description:

How it makes me feel:

Day 2:

Morning Ritual:

Description:

How it makes me feel:

Afternoon Ritual:

Description:

How it makes me feel:

Evening Ritual:

Description:

How it makes me feel:

Day 3:

Morning Ritual:

Description:

How it makes me feel:

Afternoon Ritual:

Description:

How it makes me feel:

Evening Ritual:

Description:

How it makes me feel:

Day 4:

Morning Ritual:

Description:

How it makes me feel:

Afternoon Ritual:

Description:

How it makes me feel:

Evening Ritual:

Description:

How it makes me feel:

Day 5:

Morning Ritual:

Description:

How it makes me feel:

Afternoon Ritual:

Description:

How it makes me feel:

Evening Ritual:

Description:

How it makes me feel:

Day 6:

Morning Ritual:

Description:

How it makes me feel:

Afternoon Ritual:

Description:

How it makes me feel:

Evening Ritual:

Description:

How it makes me feel:

Day 7:

Morning Ritual:

Description:

How it makes me feel:

Afternoon Ritual:

Description:

How it makes me feel:

Evening Ritual:

Description:

How it makes me feel:

Continue this pattern throughout the week, customizing each day's rituals and reflecting on how they nourish your heart, soul, and well-being. It is important to continue this every week for the year and be consistent with your daily rituals and habits.

100 Self-Care Rituals: An Abundance of Nurturing

1. Morning Meditation: Begin your day with mindful meditation, setting intentions for a positive day ahead.

2. Nature Connection: Spend time outdoors, whether it's a walk in the park, a hike, or simply enjoying your morning coffee on the balcony.

3. Gratitude Journaling: Write down three things you're grateful for each morning, cultivating a sense of appreciation.

4. Creative Expression: Dedicate time to a creative activity that brings you joy – drawing, painting, crafting, or playing a musical instrument.

5. Digital Detox: Set aside an hour to disconnect from technology and reconnect with yourself.

6. Gentle Yoga: Engage in a gentle yoga practice that nurtures your body and mind.

7. Mindful Breathing: Practice deep breathing exercises throughout the day to ground yourself.

8. Nourishing Meals: Prepare and savor a nourishing meal that fuels your body.

9. Reading Retreat: Dedicate time to read a book that inspires you.

10. Bath Ritual: Draw a warm bath with soothing salts and essential oils, creating a serene oasis.

11. Listening to Music: Listen to your favorite music and let it uplift your spirit.

12. Acts of Kindness: Perform a small act of kindness for someone else, nurturing your connection with the world.

13. Journal Reflection: Reflect on your day, noting moments of joy, challenges, and insights.

14. Expressive Dance: Put on your favorite music and let your body move freely.

15. Mindful Eating: Savor each bite of your meal, fully immersing yourself in the experience.

16. Nature Walk: Take a leisurely walk in nature, observing the beauty around you.

17. Guided Visualization: Close your eyes and immerse yourself in a guided visualization, exploring tranquil landscapes or manifesting your goals.

18. Morning Pages: Begin your day by jotting down your thoughts, stream of consciousness style, setting the tone for clarity and intention.

19. Candlelit Dinner: Create a candlelit dinner for yourself, savoring your favorite foods in an ambiance of serenity.

20. Digital Declutter: Dedicate time to declutter your digital spaces – emails, social media, and files – promoting a sense of digital well-being.

21. Letter to Your Future Self: Pen a letter to your future self, detailing your dreams and aspirations.

22. Mindful Tea Ceremony: Brew a cup of herbal tea and engage in a mindful tea ceremony, sipping slowly and savoring the flavors.

23. Sunset Meditation: Find a peaceful spot to meditate during sunset, connecting with the beauty of the changing skies.

24. Body Scan Meditation: Engage in a body scan meditation, bringing awareness and relaxation to each part of your body.

25. Random Acts of Self-Kindness: Surprise yourself with small acts of self-kindness throughout the day – a soothing cup of tea, a fragrant bouquet, or a cozy blanket.

26. Intention Setting: Begin your day by setting intentions that align with your values and goals.

27. Disconnect to Connect: Unplug from devices for an entire day, allowing yourself to fully connect with the present moment.

28. Laughter Session: Watch a comedy show, engage in laughter yoga, or share funny stories with loved ones for a dose of joyful energy.

29. Dream Journaling: Record your dreams upon waking, unraveling insights from your subconscious mind.

30. Plant Care: Spend time nurturing your indoor plants, fostering a sense of growth and renewal.

31. Visualization Board: Create a visualization board with images and words that represent your dreams and aspirations.

32. Self-Massage: Treat yourself to a relaxing self-massage with scented oils, soothing tired muscles.

33. Breathwork Practice: Engage in different breathwork exercises, such as box breathing or alternate nostril breathing, to calm your mind and body.

34. Sensory Exploration: Take a sensory journey – touch different textures, listen to soothing sounds, and indulge in aromatic experiences.

35. Volunteer: Dedicate time to a cause you care about, nurturing your sense of purpose and connection with the community.

36. Cloud Watching: Lie down and watch the clouds pass by, embracing a simple and calming nature-inspired activity.

37. Self-Compassion Letter: Write a letter to yourself from a place of self-compassion, offering kind words and understanding.

38. Mindful Walking: Take a leisurely walk, focusing your attention on the sensation of each step.

39. Artistic Expression: Try your hand at a creative outlet you've never explored before, such as pottery, sculpting, or poetry.

40. Self-Care Affirmations: Create personalized affirmations that reaffirm your worthiness and well-being.

41. Mindful Photography: Take a camera or your phone and capture the beauty around you, training your focus on the present moment.

42. Aromatherapy Bath: Infuse your bath with calming essential oils, allowing the soothing scents to relax your mind and body.

43. Dance Like Nobody's Watching: Let loose and dance freely to your favorite music, embracing the joy of movement.

44. Cloud Gazing: Lie down and gaze at the clouds, letting your mind wander as you connect with the vastness of the sky.

45. Self-Reflection Walk: Take a solitary walk, reflecting on your thoughts and feelings without distraction.

46. Random Acts of Kindness: Perform acts of kindness for strangers, nurturing your connection with humanity.

47. Mindful Eating: Eat a meal mindfully, savoring each bite and appreciating the flavors and textures.

48. Positive Affirmation Mirror: Write positive affirmations on your mirror to remind yourself of your worth every day.

49. Spa Day at Home: Create a spa-like atmosphere at home with facials, body scrubs, and soothing music.

50. Gratitude Meditation: Meditate on what you're grateful for, focusing on the abundance in your life.

51. Unplug from News: Take a break from consuming news to protect your mental and emotional well-being.

52. Listen to Nature Sounds: Immerse yourself in the sounds of nature, whether it's ocean waves, birdsong, or rustling leaves.

53. Mindful Cooking: Cook a meal mindfully, engaging all your senses as you prepare and enjoy your food.

54. Forest Bathing: Spend time in a natural setting, allowing the healing power of nature to rejuvenate your spirit.

55. Self-Love Letter: Write a letter to yourself, expressing love and acceptance for who you are.

56. Colour Therapy: Engage in coloring activities, immersing yourself in the therapeutic act of coloring.

57. Virtual Museum Tour: Explore museums and art galleries online, indulging in cultural experiences from the comfort of your home.

58. Breath of Fire: Practice the Breath of Fire technique, a powerful yogic breath that energizes and clears the mind.

59. Mindful Gardening: Tend to your garden mindfully, connecting with the earth and nurturing your plants.

60. Technology-Free Evening: Dedicate an evening to disconnecting from screens, engaging in analog activities.

61. Body Scan Yoga: Practice a body scan yoga routine, bringing awareness and relaxation to every part of your body.

62. Sunrise Watching: Wake up early to witness the sunrise, basking in the tranquil beauty of the dawn.

63. Letter to Your Past Self: Write a letter to your past self, offering comfort and wisdom to your younger self.

64. Self-Discovery Journaling: Reflect on your personal growth journey and how far you've come.

65. Self-Care Playlist: Create a playlist of songs that uplift your spirits and make you feel good.

66. Mindful Stretching: Engage in gentle stretching exercises, focusing on the sensations in your body.

67. Digital Detox Day: Dedicate a whole day to disconnecting from digital devices, embracing a tech-free experience.

68. Solo Day Trip: Take a day trip to a new place, exploring and experiencing the joy of discovery.

69. Laughter Yoga: Engage in laughter yoga exercises that release stress and promote joy.

70. Intuitive Art: Allow your intuition to guide your art creation, expressing your feelings through colors and shapes.

71. Mindful Hiking: Embark on a mindful hike, immersing yourself in the beauty of nature and grounding your senses.

72. Virtual Retreat: Attend a virtual retreat or workshop that aligns with your interests and promotes self-discovery.

73. Connect with a Friend: Spend quality time with a friend, engaging in meaningful conversation and nurturing your social connections.

74. Visualization Meditation: Practice a visualization meditation where you vividly imagine your desired outcomes and experiences.

75. Solo Movie Night: Enjoy a movie night by yourself, indulging in films that inspire and uplift you.

76. Shadow Work Journaling: Engage in shadow work by journaling about your fears, doubts, and hidden emotions.

77. Energy Cleansing: Clear your space with energy cleansing practices, such as smudging or sound healing.

78. Sensory Bath: Create a sensory bath experience with petals, candles, and soothing music.

79. Mindful Reading: Read a book mindfully, immersing yourself fully in the story and its lessons.

80. DIY Spa Treatment: Pamper yourself with a DIY spa treatment, including face masks, body scrubs, and relaxation.

81. Mindful Listening: Listen to your favorite music, focusing on the melody and lyrics to elevate your mood.

82. Morning Stretches: Begin your day with a series of gentle stretches to awaken your body and mind.

83. Moon Gazing: Spend time moon gazing, connecting with the celestial beauty and its cycles.

84. Outdoor Picnic: Have a picnic outdoors, enjoying nourishing food in the company of nature.

85. Declutter Space: Dedicate time to decluttering a space in your home, promoting a sense of clarity and organization.

86. Mindful Breathing Walk: Take a walk, syncing your breath with your steps to promote mindfulness.

87. Nature Mandala: Create a mandala using natural materials you find outdoors, fostering creativity and connection.

88. Self-Care Movie Marathon: Set aside a day for a self-care movie marathon, watching films that inspire and uplift you.

89. Mindful Crafting: Engage in a craft project, allowing your creativity to flow and your mind to find focus.

90. Evening Reflection: Reflect on your day in the evening, noting moments of growth, gratitude, and joy.

91. Guided Yoga: Practice guided yoga, a deep relaxation technique that promotes rest and rejuvenation.

92. Colorful Cooking: Cook a colorful and nourishing meal, embracing the vibrancy of fresh ingredients.

93. Dance Therapy: Dance freely to your favorite music, using movement as a form of emotional expression.

94. Unstructured Day: Dedicate a day to spontaneity, allowing yourself to do whatever feels right in the moment.

95. Self-Compassion Meditation: Practice a meditation focused on cultivating self-compassion and kindness.

96. Moonlit Walk: Take a walk under the moonlight, finding solace in the serenity of the night.

97. Solo Concert: Attend a solo concert, immersing yourself in live music that resonates with your soul.

98. Create a Vision Board: Craft a vision board that represents your dreams, goals, and aspirations.

99. Al Fresco Meal: Enjoy a meal outdoors, whether it's a picnic in the park or dining in your garden.

100. Reflect and Celebrate: Take time to reflect on your journey and celebrate the progress you've made on your self-care path.

Embrace the Rituals, Embrace Yourself

As you fill out the Table of Contents and embark on this journey of self-care rituals, remember that each moment you invest in nurturing yourself is an investment in your well-being, healing, and personal growth. These rituals are not just tasks; they're a celebration of your worthiness. By embracing these rituals, you honor the intricate tapestry of your being and create a life that's grounded in self-love, intention, and flourishing.

Chapter 4
Embracing Mindfulness and Self-Compassion: Nurturing Your Inner Sanctuary

In the fast-paced tapestry of our modern lives, mindfulness and self-compassion emerge as luminous threads that weave harmony and well-being into the fabric of our existence. This chapter delves into the profound significance of embracing mindfulness and self-compassion, exploring the scientific underpinnings that validate their transformative power. From the refuge they offer against burnout's grip to the way they anchor us in the present moment, we'll uncover the why, what, and how of integrating these practices into our lives.

The Essence of Mindfulness and Self-Compassion

In a world often marked by haste and hustle, mindfulness and self-compassion extend an invitation to pause, connect, and honor our present experiences. Mindfulness beckons us to be fully present in each moment, while self-compassion invites us to treat ourselves with the same kindness we would offer a dear friend. These practices are not mere luxuries; they are essential tools that guide us back to our inner sanctuary amidst life's storms.

Science Backing the Practices

Numerous scientific studies extol the virtues of mindfulness and self-compassion. Research published in the Journal of Applied Psychology demonstrates that mindfulness reduces stress and enhances well-being. A study by Kristin Neff, a pioneer in self-compassion research, highlights its positive impact on mental health, promoting resilience and reducing negative self-talk.

Integrating Mindfulness and Self-Compassion

Despite our bustling lives, finding moments for mindfulness and self-compassion is both essential and achievable. Start small: Dedicate a few minutes each day to focus on your breath, observe your thoughts without judgment, and treat yourself with the same kindness you would extend to a cherished friend.

When You Don't Prioritize Mindfulness and Self-Compassion

Neglecting mindfulness and self-compassion is akin to journeying through life with a dimmed lantern. The result? A path marred by burnout, stress, and a sense of detachment from the present. The consequences ripple through our well-being, relationships, and overall quality of life.

A Personal Journey of Reclamation

I, too, was ensnared in the hustle, driven by a ceaseless desire to please and achieve. It wasn't until I embraced mindfulness that I began to unravel the threads of burnout. I discovered solace in mindful walks, using them as moments of solitude to center myself. Writing and walking became my companions, helping me extract my thoughts and feelings from the labyrinth of my mind. I shifted my pace from relentless to deliberate, understanding that growth is a journey, not a sprint.

The Hare and the Tortoise: A Timeless Lesson

Like the pages of a beloved fable, the tale of the hare and the tortoise imparts its wisdom anew as time flows on. The hare's swift and relentless pace, while impressive, may lead to exhaustion and burnout. On the other hand, the tortoise's measured strides, fortified by the practice of mindfulness and self-compassion, promise a journey that's both sustainable and deeply rewarding. In this chapter, we understand that to thrive, we must honor our own pace, cherishing our well-being as we move forward. Just as the tortoise emerged victorious, you too can create your own narrative of triumph by weaving mindfulness and self-compassion into the very essence of your being.

Carving Moments of Sanctuary

Start your day slow, as if savoring the delicate dawn. Engage in mindful walks, allowing each step to root you in the present. Embrace mindful writing, releasing the burdens from your mind onto the page. Be the hare, attuned to the rhythm of your soul, pacing yourself in this grand race of life. By honoring these practices, you become the architect of your well-being, carving out moments of sanctuary amidst the symphony of existence.

Practicing Mindfulness in Daily Life: A Gift of Presence

Within the bustling currents of our daily existence lies the remarkable practice of mindfulness, a simple yet profound art that invites us to be fully present in each passing moment. In this chapter, we uncover the vital importance of practicing mindfulness and delve into the reasons it matters deeply. Building on the research we've explored earlier, we'll explore innovative ways to integrate mindfulness into the tapestry of your everyday life. Additionally, I'll share how I've embraced mindfulness in each segment of my day, fostering connection, clarity, and a heightened sense of living.

Why Mindfulness Matters

Mindfulness transcends a mere trend; it's a transformative mindset that helps us navigate life with clarity and grace. Numerous studies, including the research by the Journal of Applied Psychology and Kristin Neff, underscore its role in reducing stress, enhancing well-being, and nurturing mental resilience.

Integrating Mindfulness into Your Daily Life

Embracing mindfulness doesn't demand a radical shift; it's about infusing intention into the small moments that compose your day. Begin by anchoring yourself in the present: Feel the ground beneath your feet, savor the taste of your meals, and truly listen when someone speaks to you. Create mindfulness reminders – a soothing chime, a nature-inspired image – to gently pull you back into the now.

My Journey with Mindfulness

For me, mindfulness is a compass that guides me through each chapter of the day. In the morning, I greet the dawn with a sense of presence, sipping my coffee or herbal tea mindfully as the world awakens. Throughout work, I immerse myself fully in tasks, banishing the allure of multitasking. I carve out pockets of time for silent reflection, honouring the power of a momentary pause. Even during my evening walks, I embrace the symphony of sounds and the rhythm of my steps, finding solace in each breath. People on the Esplanade think I am scrolling little do they know I am writing my thoughts and studying something to grow my mind further.

Incorporating Mindfulness: A Daily Ritual

Morning Moments: As you rise, take a few deep breaths and set an intention for the day. Savor your morning beverage, feeling the warmth seep into your hands.

Mindful Tasks: Engage in tasks one at a time, whether it's preparing breakfast, replying to emails, or doing the dishes. Give your full attention to each action.

Breath Awareness: Throughout the day, return to your breath whenever you feel distracted or stressed. Feel the rhythm of your inhalations and exhalations.

Mindful Breaks: Dedicate short breaks to mindfulness. Close your eyes, take a few deep breaths, and scan your body for tension.

Presence in Conversations: When talking to someone, truly listen without thinking about your response. Let your focus be on understanding their words.

Mindful Meals: Before eating, take a moment to appreciate the food in front of you. Chew slowly and savor the flavors.

A Tapestry Woven with Awareness

Mindfulness isn't a grand event; it's the art of embracing life's tiniest moments with profound awareness. As you weave mindfulness into the intricate threads of your daily life, you're gifting yourself the present moment. Each breath becomes an anchor, every step a chance to recenter. By practicing mindfulness, you nurture a serene refuge amidst life's chaos and bring to life a richer, more vibrant experience.

Cultivating Self-Compassion and Letting Go of Perfectionism: Embrace Imperfection, Embrace Freedom

In the symphony of self-discovery, cultivating self-compassion and releasing the grip of perfectionism emerge as harmonious notes that resonate with our deepest selves. This chapter unveils the profound significance of nurturing self-compassion and dismantling the chains of perfectionism. Through exploring the "why" behind these practices, understanding their benefits, and experiencing their effects on mind, body, and spirit, we'll uncover the transformative power of embracing our imperfections and allowing ourselves to thrive.

The Power of Self-Compassion

In a world often critical and demanding, self-compassion becomes a haven of gentleness. It's about treating yourself with the kindness, understanding, and empathy you'd extend to a cherished friend. Why does it matter? Research shows that self-compassion is linked to reduced anxiety, depression, and stress. It's a pathway to resilience and emotional well-being.

The Ripple Effect of Letting Go of Perfectionism

Perfectionism, often seen as an aspirational trait, can paradoxically lead to burnout, stress, and a sense of inadequacy. Letting go of the need to be perfect is an act of liberation. It frees you to embrace your authentic self, fostering a sense of joy, creativity, and authenticity.

The Liberation of Imperfection

As you cultivate self-compassion and release perfectionism's grip, you'll find your spirit unburdened and your heart lighter. Your body breathes a sigh of relief, no longer constricted by the pressure to conform to an unattainable standard. The mind finds space to explore, create, and innovate. Embracing imperfection is an act of embracing freedom – it's an acknowledgment that our beauty lies in our uniqueness, not in meeting an arbitrary ideal.

Cultivating Self-Compassion: A Deeper Journey

Nurturing self-compassion is a journey that transcends mere self-care. It's an act of dismantling the inner critic, replacing judgment with understanding. It's learning to hold your struggles with gentleness, acknowledging that they're part of the human experience.

The Liberation of Letting Go

Letting go of perfectionism isn't a surrender to mediocrity; it's an invitation to wholeheartedly engage in life without the fear of falling short. It's an affirmation that your worth isn't tied to external validation. Research underscores that letting go of perfectionism leads to increased life satisfaction, fostering healthier relationships and a greater sense of well-being.

My Journey to Self-Compassion and Letting Go

I, too, embarked on this transformative journey. As I cultivated self-compassion, my inner dialogue shifted from harsh judgment to kind understanding. Letting go of perfectionism allowed me to express myself authentically, untethered from the need for approval. Through self-compassion, I found solace in my own embrace, and by releasing perfectionism's grip, I liberated myself to thrive in the beauty of imperfection.

A Transformational Pathway

As you navigate the landscape of self-compassion and let go of perfectionism, you pave a transformational pathway toward self-discovery and empowerment. You grant yourself permission to be human, to stumble and rise, and to craft a life that resonates with authenticity. Through this journey, you'll uncover an oasis of inner peace and a sanctuary of self-acceptance – a testament to the profound power of self-compassion and the liberation of embracing your imperfect, beautiful self.

Chapter 5
Building Resilience Through Self-Love: Nurturing Your Inner Sanctuary

Amid life's unpredictable tides and the ebb and flow of challenges, the sanctuary of self-love stands as an unshakeable foundation. This chapter embarks on a journey to illuminate the path of building resilience through the practice of self-love. As we delve into the essence of why self-love matters, explore its myriad benefits, and witness its transformative effects on the mind, body, and spirit, we'll uncover the profound capacity within each of us to not only weather life's storms but to emerge from them stronger, wiser, and more empowered. In a world that often demands endurance, self-love becomes the nurturing cocoon that fosters growth, healing, and unwavering resilience.

Building Resilience Through Self-Love: Nurturing Your Inner Sanctuary

Amid life's unpredictable tides and the ebb and flow of challenges, the sanctuary of self-love stands as an unshakeable foundation. This chapter embarks on a journey to illuminate the path of building resilience through the practice of self-love. As we delve into the essence of why self-love matters, explore its myriad benefits, and witness its transformative effects on the mind, body, and spirit, we'll uncover the profound capacity within each of us to not only weather life's storms but to emerge from them stronger, wiser, and more empowered. In a world that often demands endurance, self-love becomes the nurturing cocoon that fosters growth, healing, and unwavering resilience.

The Essence of Self-Love: Why It Matters

At the core of resilience lies the invaluable practice of self-love. Why does it matter? Self-love isn't just a fleeting concept; it's a cornerstone of well-being that nurtures our mental, physical, and emotional realms. By cultivating a compassionate relationship with ourselves, we construct a fortified shelter that shields us from the storms of self-doubt and criticism. This sanctuary becomes the launching pad from which we not only withstand challenges but also transcend them.

The Benefits of Embracing Self-Love

The benefits of self-love are profound and far-reaching. Mentally, self-love shifts our internal dialogue from harsh self-judgment to gentle self-acceptance, enhancing our self-esteem and fostering emotional resilience. Physically, self-love promotes a healthier lifestyle, as we prioritize our well-being through nourishing habits and restful sleep. Emotionally, self-love grants us the capacity to embrace our feelings without judgment, cultivating emotional intelligence and a profound sense of peace.

Unveiling the Transformative Power

As we walk this path of self-love, our mental landscape transforms. The cacophony of self-criticism softens, replaced by the symphony of self-acceptance. Physically, our bodies respond with vitality as we prioritize nourishment and movement as acts of self-care. Emotionally, we find ourselves anchored amidst life's turmoil, our emotional well-being fortified by the unwavering knowledge that we are deserving of love and kindness – especially from ourselves.

The Journey to Resilience: Self-Love as the Beacon

In the tapestry of resilience, self-love emerges as the guiding light that leads us through life's trials. This journey isn't just about endurance; it's about thriving. Self-love becomes the compass that guides us toward healing, growth, and transformation. As we navigate the ebb and flow of life, this foundation of self-love becomes the lighthouse that illuminates our path, reminding us that no matter the storm, we are worthy of compassion, tenderness, and unbreakable resilience.

Nurturing Self-Love and Positive Self-Talk: A Symphony of Inner Affirmation

In the journey of resilience, the harmonious duet of self-love and positive self-talk forms a potent melody that reverberates through our being. This chapter unravels the art of nurturing self-love and cultivating positive self-talk, offering you a step-by-step guide to seamlessly incorporate these practices into your life. From creating a nurturing environment to crafting empowering affirmations, we'll embark on a voyage that amplifies your self-worth and fortifies your resilience.

The Dance of Self-Love and Positive Self-Talk

Nurturing self-love isn't an abstract concept; it's a deliberate practice that shapes our inner narrative. By choosing words of encouragement, support, and kindness, we embark on a journey of positive self-talk that reverberates with the frequency of self-love. This dance between the two fosters a compassionate relationship with ourselves, a sanctuary where we can retreat during life's trials.

Implementing Self-Love and Positive Self-Talk: Step by Step

Self-Reflection: Begin by examining your inner dialogue. Notice moments of self-criticism and judgment.

Shift Your Perspective: Replace self-criticism with self-compassion. Imagine you're talking to a beloved friend and offer yourself the same kindness.

Affirmation Creation: Craft empowering affirmations that resonate with you. They should be positive, in the present tense, and aligned with your goals.

Repeat and Reinforce: Incorporate your affirmations into your daily routine. Repeat them during moments of self-doubt, and use them as anchors of positivity.

Create a Positive Environment: Surround yourself with visual cues that prompt positive self-talk. Post affirmations on your mirror, set inspirational wallpapers on your devices, and keep a gratitude journal.

Physical Environment Prompts for Positive Self-Talk

Mirror Affirmations: Write uplifting affirmations on sticky notes and place them on your mirror. They greet you each morning, setting a positive tone for the day.

Inspirational Wallpapers: Set your phone or computer wallpaper as an affirmation or an image that inspires positivity and self-love.

Gratitude Journal: Dedicate a journal to jotting down moments of gratitude and self-appreciation. This serves as a repository of positivity.

Empowering Affirmations to Live By

"I am worthy of love, compassion, and all good things in life."

"I embrace my imperfections and honor my unique journey."

"I am resilient, capable, and equipped to handle any challenge."

"I am enough as I am, and my worth is not determined by external standards."

"I choose self-love over self-criticism, kindness over judgment."

"I believe in my abilities and trust in the process of growth."

"I am the author of my story, and I choose to write it with self-love and positivity."

An Ongoing Melody of Self-Love

As you cultivate self-love and embrace positive self-talk, you're crafting an ongoing symphony of inner affirmation. With each positive thought and nurturing word, you contribute to the resonance of resilience that echoes within you. By weaving these practices into your daily life, you foster a relationship with yourself built on kindness, compassion, and unwavering support. This melody becomes your guiding light through life's journey, a reminder that you are your own greatest advocate and a testament to the beautiful synergy of self-love and positive self-talk.

Strategies to Boost Self-Esteem: Crafting a Stronger Self-Image

In the quest for resilience and inner fortitude, boosting self-esteem emerges as a vital component. This chapter unfolds a treasure trove of strategies to enhance your self-esteem, empowering you to foster a more positive self-image. Here, you'll find a comprehensive list of actionable steps, akin to a recipe for self-esteem elevation. By implementing these strategies, you'll lay the foundation for unshakeable self-worth and the ability to navigate life's challenges with unwavering confidence.

1. Practice Self-Compassion: Treat yourself with kindness, just as you would a dear friend. Challenge self-criticism with self-compassion.

2. Celebrate Achievements: Acknowledge your accomplishments, regardless of size. Celebrate your progress and efforts.

3. Positive Self-Talk: Challenge negative self-talk by countering with positive affirmations. Remind yourself of your strengths and potential.

4. Set Realistic Goals: Set achievable goals that align with your abilities and interests. Each accomplishment reinforces your self-esteem.

5. Embrace Your Uniqueness: Recognize your individuality as a source of strength. Embrace your quirks, talents, and authentic self.

6. Accept Compliments: Learn to graciously accept compliments. Internalize positive feedback and let it contribute to your self-worth.

7. Nourish Your Body: Prioritize self-care by fueling your body with nourishing food, regular exercise, and sufficient rest.

8. Practice Gratitude: Cultivate gratitude by focusing on the positive aspects of your life. Keep a gratitude journal to remind yourself of your blessings.

9. Surround Yourself with Positivity: Surround yourself with people who uplift and support you. Limit exposure to negativity.

10. Face Challenges: Tackle challenges with determination. Each success, no matter how small, bolsters your confidence.

11. Mindful Self-Reflection: Engage in mindful self-reflection to understand your thoughts, emotions, and behaviors. This self-awareness fosters growth.

12. Set Boundaries: Establish healthy boundaries in your relationships and commitments. Prioritize your well-being.

13. Develop New Skills: Pursue activities that interest you. Learning new skills and achieving mastery enhances your self-esteem.

14. Practice Self-Care: Dedicate time to activities that bring you joy and relaxation. Prioritize self-care to recharge your spirit.

15. Visualize Success: Use visualization techniques to imagine yourself succeeding in various aspects of your life. This boosts your self-confidence.

16. Seek Support: Don't hesitate to seek support from friends, family, or professionals if you're struggling with self-esteem issues.

17. Accept Imperfections: Embrace your imperfections as part of being human. Nobody is flawless, and that's what makes us beautifully unique.

18. Learn from Setbacks: View setbacks as opportunities for growth. Analyze what you can learn from challenges and apply those lessons moving forward.

19. Express Yourself: Share your thoughts, feelings, and ideas authentically. Expressing yourself fosters self-confidence.

20. Focus on Strengths: Identify your strengths and capitalize on them. Build on your areas of proficiency and competence.

21. Embrace Challenges: Approach challenges with a growth mindset. Embrace them as opportunities to learn and develop resilience.

22. Practice Self-Kindness: Be your own biggest supporter. Treat yourself with the same kindness and understanding you offer others.

23. Embody Positive Posture: Maintain confident body language, as it can influence your mental state and self-perception.

24. Limit Comparisons: Avoid comparing yourself to others. Focus on your progress and growth, rather than external benchmarks.

25. Celebrate Self-Care Victories: Acknowledge each self-care victory, no matter how small. Each act of self-care bolsters your self-esteem.

Chapter 6
Making Meaningful Experiences: Weaving Threads of Joy into Your Story

Amid the tapestry of our lives, the pursuit of meaningful experiences shines as a radiant thread that adds depth, color, and purpose. This chapter delves into the art of making meaningful experiences a cornerstone of your journey. Discover why infusing your life with these moments matters, explore the significance of their presence, and witness how they can elevate your existence to new heights. As we unravel the tapestry of their impact on overall life satisfaction, consider their role in decreasing depression and anxiety – a testament to the profound influence they wield on our well-being.

The Essence of Meaningful Experiences: Why They Matter

Meaningful experiences are the brushstrokes that paint your life with vibrant hues. They are moments that resonate, touch the heart, and nourish the soul. Why do they matter? They infuse our existence with purpose and depth, transforming the mundane into the extraordinary. By embracing meaningful experiences, we cultivate a tapestry woven with joy, fulfillment, and lasting memories.

The Importance of Making Meaning

In a world often focused on material pursuits, making meaningful experiences a priority is essential. These moments become the currency of our memories, enriching the chapters of our story with joy and significance. They remind us that life is not solely about accumulation but about weaving a narrative brimming with moments that truly matter.

Why You Should Have Meaningful Experiences in Your Life

Infusing your life with meaningful experiences isn't a luxury; it's a necessity for well-being. These moments nourish our spirit, foster connection, and enrich our emotional landscape. They act as guiding stars, steering us away from the abyss of monotony and toward the constellation of fulfillment.

Elevating Overall Life Satisfaction

The impact of meaningful experiences on overall life satisfaction is profound. Research has shown that engaging in activities that align with our values and bring joy contributes significantly to our sense of well-being. These experiences elevate our mood, enrich our relationships, and ignite a sense of purpose that resonates far beyond the moment itself.

A Ray of Hope: Decreasing Depression and Anxiety

Beyond Blue Australia emphasizes the therapeutic role of meaningful experiences in decreasing depression and anxiety. Engaging in activities that evoke joy, connection, and a sense of accomplishment can be a potent remedy for the struggles of mental health. Meaningful experiences shine as beacons of light, guiding us through the darkness and helping us find solace, even in the midst of challenges.

Crafting a Life Enriched by Meaning

As you journey through life, remember that making meaningful experiences isn't just an option; it's an invitation to infuse your story with purpose, joy, and fulfillment. By weaving these threads of significance into your narrative, you're crafting a life that's not only rich in memories but also brimming with emotional resilience. The moments you create are the legacy you leave behind – a testament to the profound impact of embracing the beauty and power of meaningful experiences.

Making Meaningful Experiences: Finding Joy In Small Moments

Amidst the hustle and bustle of life, the pursuit of meaningful experiences emerges as a tapestry woven with threads of joy. In this section, we delve into the profound significance of crafting these moments and explore the transformative benefits they bring. From uncovering the steps to infuse your life with joy to understanding why it's essential to prioritize these experiences, we'll illuminate how joy serves as the highest frequency, infusing every corner of your existence with radiant energy.

Why Meaningful Experiences Matter

Meaningful experiences are the kaleidoscope of colors that enrich the canvas of our lives. Each vibrant moment adds depth, texture, and purpose to the tapestry of existence. These experiences remind us that life isn't solely about the routine; it's about weaving a narrative studded with moments that evoke joy, fulfillment, and a sense of wonder.

The Transformative Benefits of Joyful Moments

The benefits of crafting meaningful experiences are as diverse as the experiences themselves. These moments elevate our mood, foster connection with ourselves and others, and amplify our overall well-being. Engaging in activities that bring joy can reduce stress, enhance creativity, and fortify our emotional resilience in the face of challenges.

Steps to Infuse Your Life with Joy

Reflect on Passions: Identify activities that ignite your passion and curiosity. These are the wellsprings of joy waiting to be explored.

Embrace Novelty: Break free from routine by trying new things. Novelty sparks excitement and can lead to discovering new sources of joy.

Prioritize Playfulness: Allow yourself to be playful and childlike. Engaging in playful activities can spark joy and bring a sense of carefree delight.

Create Moments of Connection: Engage in activities that foster connection with loved ones. Shared experiences often amplify the joy felt.

Seek Beauty in Everyday: Train your eye to find beauty in ordinary moments – a sunrise, a blooming flower, or the laughter of a child.

Why Joy Matters: Elevating Your Frequency

Joy isn't just an emotion; it's the highest frequency and energy we can cultivate. When we engage in joyful activities, we're aligning ourselves with a positive and vibrant energy that permeates our being. This energy ripples through our thoughts, emotions, and actions, elevating our overall state of being.

Bringing Joy into Your Life: A Symphony of Possibilities

Nature Immersion: Spend time in nature, whether it's a leisurely hike, a walk in the park, or a day at the beach.

Creative Expression: Engage in creative endeavors that light up your soul – painting, writing, dancing, or playing music.

Savoring Culinary Delights: Experiment with cooking or dining at a new restaurant to savor delightful flavors.

Exploring New Places: Travel to new destinations and immerse yourself in different cultures and experiences.

Acts of Kindness: Perform acts of kindness for others, as the joy derived from giving is both profound and enduring.

Connecting with Passion: Revisit hobbies and passions you may have neglected over time, reigniting the joy they bring.

A Tapestry Woven with Joy

As you weave joy into the fabric of your life through meaningful experiences, you're crafting a tapestry of beauty, vibrancy, and vitality. These moments, large or small, become the brushstrokes of a life well-lived, resonating with a frequency that uplifts not only you but those around you. Embrace the power of joy as the guiding star on your journey, and watch as your existence becomes a symphony of laughter, connection, and profound fulfillment.

Pursuing Passion Projects and Hobbies: Nurturing Your Creative Soul

In the landscape of personal growth and joy, the pursuit of passion projects and hobbies emerges as a fertile ground for self-expression and fulfillment. This section dives deep into the realm of cultivating creativity, exploring why these pursuits matter, and providing you with a roadmap on how to embark on your journey. From ideation to execution, we'll guide you through the process of infusing your life with projects that ignite your passions and hobbies that enliven your spirit.

Why Pursuing Passion Projects and Hobbies Matters

Passion projects and hobbies aren't mere diversions; they're avenues of self-discovery and creative expression. Engaging in these pursuits invigorates your mind, nourishes your soul, and enriches your emotional landscape. They remind you of your innate creativity and offer a channel for exploring new skills and interests.

Crafting Your Passion Project: How to Begin

Identify Your Passion: Reflect on what truly excites you. What activities or subjects bring you joy? It could be anything from writing to woodworking, painting to photography.

Set Clear Goals: Define your project's purpose and objectives. What do you want to achieve through this endeavor? Setting clear goals will keep you motivated.

Plan Your Approach: Break down your project into manageable steps. Create a timeline and allocate time each week to work on it.

Gather Resources: Collect the tools, materials, and information you need for your project. This ensures a smooth and enjoyable journey.

Stay Committed: Consistency is key. Dedicate regular time to your project, even if it's just a small step each day.

100 Passion Project Ideas

Restore vintage cars or motorcycles.

Start a community garden.

Organize local charity events.

Teach a cooking or baking class.

Create an online course in your field of expertise.

Design and sell custom-made jewelry.

Build a treehouse or backyard oasis.

Learn a new language and offer language lessons.

Write and illustrate a children's book.

Become a certified life coach.

Volunteer at an animal shelter or wildlife sanctuary.

Start a travel blog documenting your adventures.

Design and plant a sustainable garden.

Host themed dinner parties or culinary events.

Learn woodworking and craft custom wooden items.

Develop a fitness or wellness program.

Paint and sell your artwork online.

Train to become a yoga or meditation instructor.

Create an online course on personal development.

Start a YouTube channel for DIY home projects.

Learn calligraphy and offer personalized services.

Record and produce your own music album.

Become a certified nutritionist or health coach.

Write a memoir or personal growth book.

Start a virtual book club or reading group.

Build and maintain birdhouses or feeders.

Organize local clean-up initiatives.

Host online workshops on mindfulness.

Learn to sew and create fashion accessories.

Train and compete in a sporting event.

Start a blog on mental health and well-being.

Create personalized digital art commissions.

Develop a gardening or horticulture project.

Start a podcast on eco-friendly living.

Volunteer to teach art to underprivileged youth.

Craft and sell handmade candles or soaps.

Launch a website on sustainable living.

Design and create your own board games.

Learn pottery or ceramics and sell your creations.

Develop a local art exhibition or gallery.

Host workshops on stress management and relaxation.

Start a YouTube channel for cooking tutorials.

Train and participate in a marathon or triathlon.

Create a virtual reality experience or game.

Learn to dance and offer dance lessons.

Start a blog on mindfulness and meditation.

Build and maintain a community composting program.

Organize local fundraising events for charity.

Develop a line of eco-friendly products.

Volunteer as a mentor or coach for youth.

Design and create personalized stationery.

Start a podcast discussing sustainable living.

Learn coding and develop your own software.

Train to become a certified fitness instructor.

Host workshops on creative writing.

Develop a nature photography exhibit.

Create a fashion brand using sustainable materials.

Volunteer for local environmental clean-ups.

Start a YouTube channel focused on DIY projects.

Train and participate in a dance competition.

Build and launch a small-scale hydroponic garden.

Organize workshops on plant-based cooking.

Develop a series of self-help videos.

Start a blog on eco-friendly home design.

Learn woodworking and build furniture for charity.

Volunteer at a local community center.

Host workshops on personal finance management.

Create and sell eco-friendly home products.

Develop a mindfulness and meditation app.

Learn photography and offer portrait sessions.

Start a YouTube channel for travel vlogs.

Train and compete in a martial arts tournament.

Organize charity walks or runs.

Develop an online platform for eco-conscious products.

Start a podcast on sustainable fashion.

Train and participate in a painting competition.

Create and sell handmade pottery.

Develop a series of gardening tutorials.

Host workshops on creative expression.

Start a blog on holistic health practices.

Train and compete in a chess tournament.

Volunteer to teach music or art to children.

Design and build energy-efficient homes.

Develop a virtual reality experience for education.

Start a YouTube channel for home renovation tips.

Train and participate in a photography contest.

Organize community sports leagues.

Develop an online platform for sustainable travel.

Start a podcast on minimalism and decluttering.

Train and compete in a baking or cooking competition.

Create and sell handmade skincare products.

Develop a series of outdoor adventure workshops.

Host workshops on holistic nutrition.

Start a blog on ethical fashion choices.

Train and participate in a gardening competition.

Volunteer to teach fitness or dance to seniors.

Design and build energy-efficient appliances.

Develop a virtual reality experience for history education.

Start a YouTube channel for eco-friendly living tips.

Train and participate in a knitting or crochet contest.

Let your passion guide you toward a fulfilling project that aligns with your interests and values. Your journey toward personal growth and contribution to the world awaits!

Embracing Enriching Hobbies: Where to Begin

Explore Curiosities: Think about hobbies you've always wanted to try. Consider your interests in art, sports, crafts, or other creative pursuits.

Start Small: Begin with a simple hobby that doesn't require a significant investment of time or resources.

Join a Community: Engage with local clubs or online groups dedicated to your chosen hobby. This creates a supportive environment for learning and growth.

Practice Regularly: Dedicate consistent time to your hobby to develop proficiency and enjoyment.

Experiment and Evolve: Don't be afraid to try different hobbies until you find the one that resonates with you.

100 Hobby Ideas to Explore

Gardening: Cultivate a green thumb and create your own oasis of plants and flowers, whether in a small balcony garden or a spacious backyard.

Cooking: Dive into the culinary world, experiment with new recipes, and explore various cuisines to delight your taste buds.

Yoga: Embark on a journey of self-discovery and physical wellness through yoga, embracing mindfulness and flexibility.

Pottery: Unleash your creativity by molding clay into functional or decorative pieces of art, experiencing the therapeutic joy of sculpting.

Calligraphy: Master the art of beautiful handwriting, turning words into exquisite pieces of artistry with elegant strokes.

Birdwatching: Immerse yourself in the world of birds, observe their behavior, and learn to identify various species in your area.

Astronomy: Gaze at the stars, planets, and celestial bodies, studying the cosmos and deepening your understanding of the universe.

Hiking: Connect with nature and explore scenic trails, discovering breathtaking landscapes and fostering a sense of adventure.

Origami: Transform sheets of paper into intricate 3D creations through the ancient Japanese art of origami.

Geocaching: Combine outdoor exploration with treasure hunting by using GPS coordinates to find hidden caches around your area.

Scrapbooking: Preserve memories creatively by assembling photos, memorabilia, and decorative elements into personalized scrapbooks.

Rollerblading: Glide through your surroundings on rollerblades, enjoying a dynamic and invigorating physical activity.

Candle Making: Craft your own scented and decorative candles, infusing your space with soothing fragrances.

Puzzle Solving: Challenge your mind with various puzzles, from crosswords and Sudoku to jigsaw puzzles and brain teasers.

Beekeeping: Immerse yourself in the world of bees, learn about their intricate societies, and harvest your own honey.

Archery: Master the art of precision by learning archery, enhancing focus and patience while honing your accuracy.

Playing Board Games: Indulge in strategic and competitive fun by playing a variety of board games with friends and family.

Interior Decorating: Express your creativity by redesigning and arranging spaces to create harmonious and visually pleasing environments.

Wood Carving: Transform raw wood into intricate sculptures or functional items, learning to shape and detail with precision.

Volunteering: Give back to your community by dedicating time to volunteer activities that align with your interests and values.

Photography: Capture moments and memories through the lens of a camera, experimenting with different subjects and techniques.

Knitting or Crocheting: Create cozy garments, blankets, and accessories using knitting needles or crochet hooks.

Painting: Express your creativity on canvas with various painting mediums, from acrylics and watercolors to oils.

Reading: Immerse yourself in the worlds of fiction, non-fiction, or poetry, gaining knowledge and inspiration from the written word.

Running: Embark on a journey of physical fitness and mental resilience by taking up running and setting personal goals.

Learning a Musical Instrument: Develop your musical talents by picking up a musical instrument like the guitar, piano, or violin.

Writing: Express your thoughts, ideas, and stories through writing, whether it's journaling, blogging, or creative writing.

Dancing: Channel your energy into different dance styles, from salsa and hip-hop to ballet and contemporary.

Model Building: Assemble intricate models of cars, planes, ships, or architectural structures, honing your attention to detail.

Baking: Explore the art of baking, experimenting with different recipes to create delicious pastries, bread, and desserts.

Fishing: Find tranquility by casting a line and immersing yourself in the serene world of fishing.

Rock Climbing: Challenge your physical strength and mental focus by scaling rocks and indoor climbing walls.

Sewing: Craft your own clothing, accessories, or home decor items by learning the art of sewing.

Meditation: Explore inner peace and self-awareness through meditation, cultivating mindfulness and reducing stress.

Cycling: Enjoy the outdoors while cycling through trails or roads, staying active and embracing the thrill of speed.

Learning a New Language: Dive into a new culture by learning a foreign language, broadening your horizons and communication skills.

Creative Journaling: Combine writing, drawing, and artistic elements to create visually appealing and introspective journal entries.

Photography Editing: Enhance your photography skills by exploring post-processing techniques and editing software.

Card Making: Create personalized and artistic greeting cards for various occasions, adding a personal touch to your sentiments.

Playing a New Sport: Try your hand at a sport you've never played before, embracing the challenge and growth it brings.

Brewing Your Own Coffee or Tea: Dive into the world of beverages by learning the art of brewing your own coffee or tea blends.

Collecting: Develop a collection of items that fascinate you, whether it's stamps, coins, vintage toys, or rare books.

Home DIY Projects: Tackle do-it-yourself home improvement projects, from renovating rooms to creating custom furniture.

Blogging: Share your thoughts, expertise, or experiences by starting a blog on a topic that resonates with you.

Golfing: Improve your swing and precision on the golf course, enjoying the outdoors and friendly competition.

Pet Training: Develop a bond with your furry friend by learning training techniques and teaching them new tricks.

Online Gaming: Explore virtual worlds and engage in multiplayer experiences by delving into online gaming.

Candlelight Dinners: Create a cozy and romantic ambiance by cooking candlelit dinners for yourself or loved ones.

Genealogy Research: Uncover your family's history and trace your ancestry through genealogical research.

Creating Digital Art: Express your artistic side using digital tools, creating digital paintings, illustrations, and designs.

Hiking Photography: Combine your love for hiking and photography to capture stunning nature shots during your hikes.

Camping: Embrace the great outdoors by setting up camp, connecting with nature, and stargazing.

Kayaking or Canoeing: Paddle through calm waters, rivers, or lakes while enjoying the tranquility of nature.

Learning Magic Tricks: Master the art of illusion and magic tricks to entertain and amaze friends and family.

Sudoku and Crossword Puzzles: Engage your mind and challenge your problem-solving skills with these brain-teasing puzzles.

Home Brewing: Experiment with brewing your own beer, cider, or other beverages to savor unique flavors.

Martial Arts: Develop physical strength and discipline while learning techniques from various martial arts disciplines.

Outdoor Painting: Set up your easel outdoors and paint landscapes, embracing the beauty of the natural world.

Cycling Tours: Embark on longer cycling journeys to explore new areas and challenge yourself physically.

Remote Control (RC) Vehicles: Dive into the world of remote control cars, planes, boats, or drones for hours of fun.

Sculpting: Shape and mold materials like clay, wood, or stone to create three-dimensional sculptures.

Baking and Decorating: Take your baking skills to the next level by focusing on intricate cake decorating techniques.

Nature Journaling: Combine art and nature by documenting your outdoor experiences through sketches and observations.

Wine Tasting: Develop an appreciation for different wines by exploring various types and regions.

Photography Expeditions: Plan photography trips to specific locations or landmarks to capture stunning images.

Collecting Vinyl Records: Dive into the world of music history by building a collection of vintage vinyl records.

Learning Martial Arts: Master self-defense techniques and cultivate discipline through martial arts training.

Creative Writing: Explore short stories, poetry, or creative essays to nurture your literary creativity.

Cross-Stitching or Embroidery: Create intricate designs on fabric using needle and thread, expressing your artistic flair.

Baking Artisan Bread: Dive into the art of bread making by experimenting with different types of artisanal loaves.

Outdoor Fitness Workouts: Take your workouts outside by doing yoga, calisthenics, or high-intensity interval training.

Restoring Furniture: Give new life to old furniture by refinishing, repainting, and restoring pieces to their former glory.

Astrophotography: Capture stunning images of celestial objects like planets, stars, and galaxies using photography.

Creative Podcasting: Start a podcast exploring niche topics or interviewing experts in your chosen field.

Rock Collecting and Polishing: Discover unique rocks, minerals, and gems and turn them into polished works of art.

Learning Martial Arts: Explore martial arts forms like taekwondo, kung fu, or karate to develop self-defense skills.

Urban Exploration (Urbex): Explore abandoned buildings, tunnels, and sites to uncover hidden histories.

Woodworking: Craft intricate pieces of furniture, sculptures, or decorative items using woodworking techniques.

Home Renovation: Embark on larger-scale home improvement projects, remodeling rooms or spaces.

Aquarium Keeping: Create and maintain a vibrant underwater world by keeping and caring for a variety of fish and aquatic plants.

Horseback Riding: Experience the beauty of equestrian activities by learning horseback riding and connecting with these majestic animals.

Bonsai Cultivation: Master the art of cultivating miniature trees, shaping them into intricate and captivating forms.

Learning Sign Language: Expand your communication skills by learning sign language and fostering inclusivity.

Baking Artisan Pastries: Experiment with crafting exquisite pastries, from delicate croissants to flaky danishes.

Ceramic Painting: Decorate ceramic pieces with your own designs and colors, creating functional and decorative art.

Indoor Rock Climbing: Scale indoor climbing walls to improve your climbing skills and physical strength.

Bookbinding: Craft your own personalized journals, sketchbooks, and notebooks through the art of bookbinding.

Soap Making: Create handmade soaps with various scents, colors, and designs, exploring the chemistry of soap creation.

Jewelry Making: Craft unique and personalized jewelry pieces using beads, wire, and various materials.

Nature Photography: Capture the beauty of the natural world through your camera lens, focusing on landscapes and wildlife.

Scuba Diving: Explore underwater realms by becoming a certified scuba diver and discovering marine life.

Upcycling and Repurposing: Transform discarded items into functional or artistic creations, embracing sustainability.

Sketchnoting: Combine sketching and note-taking to create visual summaries of concepts, talks, or lectures.

Silversmithing: Learn to work with silver and other metals to create intricate jewelry pieces and decorative items.

Mosaic Art: Assemble colorful tiles, glass, and other materials to create stunning mosaic designs on various surfaces.

Vintage Clothing Restoration: Restore and refashion vintage clothing pieces, embracing fashion history and sustainability.

Puppetry: Create and manipulate puppets to tell stories and engage in artistic performances.

Feng Shui Design: Explore the ancient art of arranging spaces harmoniously to enhance the flow of energy and create balanced environments.

Outdoor Sketching: Set up your easel outdoors and capture the beauty of nature through sketches and drawings.

Perfume Making: Craft your own signature scents by blending essential oils and creating unique perfumes.

Learning Astrology: Dive into the world of astrology, studying the positions and movements of celestial bodies to gain insights into personality traits and life events.

Chapter 7
Redefining Success and Setting Boundaries: Crafting a Life Aligned with Your Values

In the pursuit of well-being and fulfillment, the journey of redefining success and setting healthy boundaries stands as a transformative path. In this section, we delve into the profound importance of this dual endeavor, exploring the benefits they bestow upon your emotional landscape. By understanding the essence of boundaries and reshaping your perception of success, you'll cultivate a life that aligns with your values and preserves your well-being.

Why Redefining Success and Setting Boundaries Matter

The conventional notions of success often lead us astray from our true desires and well-being. By redefining success, you reclaim the power to shape your journey on your terms. Equally important, setting boundaries ensures that your relationships and commitments align with your values, preserving your emotional and mental equilibrium.

The Transformative Benefits of Boundary Setting

Setting boundaries establishes a framework of respect and self-care. It prevents burnout, fosters positive relationships, and enhances your emotional well-being. As you communicate your limits clearly, you create a space where your needs are acknowledged and your energy is preserved.

Understanding Boundaries: What Are They?

Boundaries are the emotional and physical limits you establish to protect your well-being and maintain healthy relationships. They help you manage your time, energy, and emotions, allowing you to navigate life's complexities with grace and assertiveness.

Redefining Success: Shifting Your Perspective

Redefining success involves moving beyond society's narrow definitions and discovering what truly resonates with you. Success becomes a holistic tapestry woven from moments of joy, purpose, meaningful relationships, and personal growth.

Refining Your Definition of Success

Reflect on Your Values: Identify what truly matters to you. Is it family, self-care, personal growth, or creative pursuits?

Set Personal Goals: Define goals that reflect your values. Aim for achievements that resonate with your intrinsic desires.

Prioritize Balance: Strive for balance in various aspects of life, including work, relationships, and self-care.

Setting Boundaries: A Spectrum of Self-Care

With Friends:

Share personal details that are comfortable.

Communicate your needs and preferences.

Politely decline invitations if you're not up for it.

With Family:

Establish open communication about your boundaries.

Express your emotions calmly if someone crosses a boundary.

Schedule regular family time without feeling obligated.

With Colleagues:

Define your working hours and stick to them.

Politely decline work tasks outside your responsibilities.

Be assertive when addressing unwanted behavior.

With Acquaintances:

Share surface-level details without delving into personal matters.

Politely decline sharing when you're not comfortable.

Keep conversations light and positive.

With People in Shops:

Be courteous while declining assistance if you don't need it.

Set boundaries around personal space.

Politely refuse offers or suggestions you're not interested in.

By embarking on the journey of redefining success and setting boundaries, you're sculpting a life that's aligned with your values and well-being. These practices empower you to embrace your authenticity, honor your needs, and cultivate relationships that uplift and respect your boundaries. As you navigate the ever-changing currents of life, you'll find that the pursuit of success becomes a pursuit of happiness, and boundaries become the guardians of your emotional equilibrium.

Rethinking Success: Quality vs. Quantity - The Art of Discernment

In the realm of personal growth and fulfillment, the paradigm of redefining success shifts our focus from quantity to quality, revealing the transformative power of discernment. This section delves into the essence of this shift, exploring its significance in the pursuit of a purposeful life. By understanding the nuances of quality versus quantity, you'll embark on a journey to reshape your perception of success and infuse your reality with deeper meaning.

Understanding Rethinking Success: The Pursuit of Depth

At its core, rethinking success involves moving beyond the superficial metrics of achievement and embracing a more profound quest for meaning and fulfillment. It's about recalibrating our aspirations to prioritize depth, purpose, and lasting impact over sheer quantity.

Why Rethinking Success Matters

In a world often enamored by external accolades and material accumulation, rethinking success serves as a compass that directs us toward a more soul-enriching path. This shift enables us to navigate life's journey with intention, aligning our goals with our values and desires.

Quality vs. Quantity: Navigating the Dichotomy

Quality: Focuses on the intrinsic value, excellence, and depth of experiences, relationships, and achievements. Quality-driven pursuits resonate deeply with our authentic selves and lead to lasting satisfaction.

Quantity: Emphasizes accumulation, quantity of possessions, and ticking off accomplishments without necessarily considering their depth or alignment with our values.

Rethinking Success in Your Reality: Steps to Embrace Depth

Identify Your Core Values: Reflect on the values that truly matter to you. What aspects of life bring you the most joy and fulfillment?

Set Intentional Goals: Craft goals that align with your values and resonate with your authentic self. Prioritize depth over mere completion.

Embrace Mindful Choices: Make deliberate choices that enhance your well-being, relationships, and personal growth, rather than following societal norms.

Cultivate Present-Moment Awareness: Practice mindfulness to fully experience each moment. It's in the present that we discover the depth of life's richness.

Reflective Questions for Life and Business

For Life:

What brings me the deepest sense of joy and fulfillment in my life?

Are there areas where I've prioritized quantity over quality? How can I recalibrate?

How can I infuse more purpose and depth into my daily routines and interactions?

For Business:

Are my professional pursuits aligned with my core values?

How can I deliver higher value and quality to my clients, customers, or audience?

What actions can I take to ensure that my business goals reflect depth and authenticity, rather than mere numbers?

As you embark on the journey of rethinking success through the lens of quality versus quantity, you're navigating a transformative path that elevates your perspective and nurtures your sense of purpose. By embracing depth, you cultivate a life imbued with authenticity, meaning, and fulfillment. With each intentional choice and reflective question, you're crafting a reality that celebrates the richness of quality experiences, relationships, and accomplishments, leading you to a more purposeful and contented existence.

Setting Healthy Boundaries to Prevent Burnout: Nurturing Your Well-Being

In the symphony of self-care, the practice of setting healthy boundaries emerges as a harmonious chord that prevents burnout and preserves your well-being. This section delves into the essence of healthy boundaries, guiding you through their implementation and unveiling the transformative impact they wield. By understanding the power of boundaries and their role in preventing burnout, you'll create a protective shield that allows you to navigate life's demands with grace and vitality.

Understanding Healthy Boundaries: Building Emotional Fences

Healthy boundaries are the invisible lines you draw to define your limits and safeguard your well-being. They allow you to distinguish between your responsibilities and those of others, preserving your energy and emotional equilibrium.

Why Setting Healthy Boundaries Matters

In a world of constant demands and expectations, setting healthy boundaries serves as an act of self-preservation. It's a declaration that your well-being matters and that you deserve respect, both from yourself and from others. Without healthy boundaries, you risk depleting your energy, leading to burnout, stress, and emotional exhaustion.

Implementing Healthy Boundaries: A Blueprint for Well-Being

Reflect on Your Needs: Identify the areas of your life where you need to set boundaries. Is it your work-life balance, personal relationships, or digital engagement?

Clearly Communicate: Articulate your boundaries assertively and clearly. Use "I" statements to express your needs and limits without blame.

Stay Consistent: Once you've established boundaries, maintain consistency. Don't waver or compromise unless it aligns with your well-being.

Prioritize Self-Care: Allocate time for self-care and recharge. This communicates to yourself and others that your well-being is non-negotiable.

The Role of Boundaries in Preventing Burnout

Setting healthy boundaries is a cornerstone in preventing burnout. By safeguarding your time, energy, and emotional resources, you ensure that you have the capacity to navigate life's challenges without sacrificing your well-being.

In Professional Life: Boundaries prevent work from permeating your personal life. Define your working hours, avoid overcommitting, and learn to say no when necessary.

In Personal Relationships: Establish boundaries that protect your emotional space. Communicate when you need time alone or when you can't engage in certain conversations.

In Digital Interactions: Limit your screen time and create tech-free zones. Set boundaries around responding to messages promptly, ensuring you have time for focused work and relaxation.

Avoiding Burnout Through Boundaries: A Shield of Resilience

Prioritize Self-Care: Setting boundaries ensures that you have the time and space for self-care practices that replenish your energy.

Preserve Emotional Energy: Boundaries prevent emotional overextension, preserving your emotional well-being and preventing emotional burnout.

Nurture Work-Life Balance: Healthy boundaries create a clear separation between work and personal life, preventing work-related burnout.

Empower Assertiveness: Setting boundaries strengthens your assertiveness muscle, empowering you to advocate for your well-being.

Enhance Resilience: By preventing burnout, healthy boundaries enhance your resilience, allowing you to weather life's storms with grace and strength.

As you weave the tapestry of your life, remember that setting healthy boundaries is not an act of selfishness, but an act of self-care. It's a commitment to preserving your well-being, nurturing your energy, and preventing the insidious grip of burnout. By embracing the power of healthy boundaries, you're forging a path toward greater vitality, emotional resilience, and a more balanced and fulfilled existence.

CHAPTER 8
Gratitude Practice and Prayer: Nourishing the Soul

In the symphony of self-care, the practices of gratitude and prayer emerge as melodious notes that resonate deeply with the soul. This section explores the transformative power of these practices, guiding you through the essence of gratitude and the nourishing embrace of prayer. By understanding the significance of these practices, you'll embark on a journey to nurture your well-being, foster mindfulness, and reignite your connection to spirituality.

Understanding Gratitude Practice and Prayer: A Harmonious Blend

Gratitude Practice: This is a deliberate and mindful act of acknowledging and appreciating the blessings, big and small, that grace your life. It's a way to shift your focus from what's lacking to what's present, cultivating a positive and appreciative mindset.

Prayer: This is a personal dialogue with a higher power, the universe, or your inner self. It's a form of meditation that allows you to express your thoughts, wishes, and gratitude, fostering a sense of connection and spirituality.

Why Cultivating Gratitude and Prayer Matters

In the hustle of modern life, the art of gratitude and the solace of prayer often get overshadowed by the noise of busyness and distractions. Yet, these practices hold the key to nurturing your emotional well-being, promoting mindfulness, and inviting spirituality into your life.

Nourishing the Soul Through Gratitude

Cultivating Positivity: Gratitude shifts your focus from the negative to the positive, infusing your mindset with optimism and appreciation.

Enhancing Mental Health: Regular gratitude practice has been linked to reduced stress, anxiety, and depression, fostering emotional resilience.

Fostering Connection: Gratitude nurtures relationships by creating an atmosphere of appreciation, enhancing your emotional bonds with others.

The Solace of Prayer

Fostering Inner Peace: Prayer provides a sanctuary for inner reflection, allowing you to find solace amidst life's chaos.

Deepening Mindfulness: Engaging in prayer encourages present-moment awareness, grounding you in the here and now.

Inviting Spiritual Connection: Prayer opens a channel to connect with your spirituality, a higher power, or the universe, nurturing a sense of purpose.

Rediscovering Mindfulness and Spirituality

In the race for productivity and achievement, the practices of gratitude and prayer have often been sidelined. Modern life's fast pace and constant distractions have disconnected us from the present moment and our spiritual essence. However, it's never too late to reclaim these practices and reintegrate them into your daily life.

Bringing Gratitude and Prayer Back into Your Life

Create Rituals: Set aside specific times for gratitude practice and prayer. Make them part of your morning or bedtime routine.

Use Reminders: Place visual cues around your environment to remind you to pause and express gratitude or engage in prayer.

Journaling: Maintain a gratitude journal to chronicle your blessings, and keep a prayer journal to document your conversations with the universe.

Mindful Moments: Integrate moments of mindfulness into your day. Use these pauses to express gratitude and engage in silent prayer.

As you embrace the practices of gratitude and prayer, you're nurturing the depths of your soul and creating space for mindfulness and spirituality. These practices are not rigid obligations but rather expressions of self-care and connection. By infusing your life with gratitude and prayer, you're sowing the seeds of positivity, mindfulness, and spiritual growth, creating a harmonious symphony that resonates within and enriches every facet of your being.

Cultivating Gratitude for Well-Being: A Path to Radiant Living

In the garden of personal growth, the seeds of gratitude flourish into vibrant blooms that nourish the soil of well-being. This section delves into the profound significance of cultivating gratitude, unraveling why it matters and how it impacts your overall sense of well-being. By understanding the transformative power of gratitude, you'll embark on a journey that elevates your outlook on life, enhances your emotional landscape, and fosters a radiant state of being.

Why Cultivating Gratitude Matters

Gratitude isn't just a fleeting emotion; it's a profound state of awareness that infuses your life with richness and depth. By actively cultivating gratitude, you open yourself to the profound beauty and abundance that surrounds you, creating a ripple effect that touches every facet of your existence.

The Profound Importance of Gratitude

Enhanced Perspective: Gratitude shifts your focus from what's missing to what's present. It's a lens through which you view the world's beauty, even amidst challenges.

Emotional Resilience: When you cultivate gratitude, you build a reservoir of positivity that acts as a shield against negativity and stress. This resilience bolsters your emotional well-being.

Strengthened Relationships: Gratitude nurtures connections by fostering appreciation and empathy. It's a powerful tool to create a harmonious and supportive social network.

Impacts on Well-Being: The Science Behind Gratitude

Research has shown that practicing gratitude has tangible benefits for your well-being. It's linked to lower stress levels, reduced anxiety, improved sleep quality, and increased overall life satisfaction. When you cultivate gratitude, you're essentially rewiring your brain to focus on the positive aspects of life, leading to improved mental and emotional health.

Embracing Gratitude as a Way of Life

Gratitude Journaling: Dedicate a few minutes each day to jot down things you're grateful for. This practice deepens your awareness of the blessings in your life.

Mindful Moments: Infuse your day with moments of mindful gratitude. Pause to appreciate the beauty around you, the taste of your food, or the warmth of the sun on your skin.

Express Your Thanks: Don't hesitate to express your gratitude to others. A heartfelt thank you can brighten someone's day and foster positive connections.

Shift Negativity: Whenever negativity creeps in, consciously redirect your focus to something you're grateful for. This helps reframe your perspective.

Practice Self-Compassion: Extend gratitude to yourself for the efforts you make and the progress you achieve. Treat yourself with kindness and appreciation.

Cultivating gratitude isn't just about saying "thank you." It's about fostering an attitude of awe and appreciation for the blessings that enrich your life, both big and small. By embracing gratitude as a way of life, you're sowing seeds of positivity that blossom into a lush garden of well-being. Each expression of gratitude becomes a stepping stone on your journey to a more fulfilled and contented existence.

Incorporating Gratitude into Daily Life: A Transformative Practice

The journey to well-being often threads through the fabric of daily routines and choices. One such practice that has the power to reinvigorate your perspective and transform your world is the art of gratitude. In this section, we'll delve into the essence of incorporating gratitude into your everyday life, drawing inspiration from personal experiences and sharing insights on how this practice can help overcome burnout.

My Journey with Gratitude: A Shift from Negativity to Blessings

The path from burnout to well-being can often seem daunting, but gratitude acted as a compass that guided me out of the shadows. Once a victim of burnout, I realized that changing my perspective was pivotal. By shifting my focus from the negative to the blessings, I began to witness a remarkable change in my life.

Starting the Day with Positivity

When the sun rises, I greet the day with positivity. The first thoughts that shape my morning are those of gratitude. Instead of waking up worried and anxious, I remind myself to embrace the day with a heart full of appreciation. This sets the tone for the hours ahead, infusing each moment with a sense of purpose and joy.

The Power of Evening Reflection

As the day winds down, I take a few moments to reflect on its events. Instead of dwelling on the challenges, I focus on the blessings that have unfolded. This practice of evening reflection has become my anchor, allowing me to retire to bed with a positive mind. After all, as I discovered, how we wake up often shapes the way we navigate the entire day.

Reframing the Mind for a Positive Outlook

It's easy to be consumed by worries and negative thoughts, especially during trying times. However, I've learned that reframing the mind is a practice that cultivates resilience and well-being. By consciously steering our thoughts towards gratitude, we create a shield against negativity and embrace the beauty that exists even amidst challenges.

Embarking on the Gratitude Journey

Incorporating gratitude into daily life doesn't require grand gestures. It's about infusing your routine with small, intentional acts of thankfulness. Here are a few ways to start:

Morning Gratitude: As you wake up, take a moment to express gratitude for the new day and the opportunities it brings.

Gratitude Journaling: Keep a journal where you jot down things you're grateful for. This practice fosters mindfulness and amplifies your appreciation.

Gratitude Affirmations: Create positive affirmations that remind you to focus on the blessings in your life. Repeat them throughout the day.

Pause and Appreciate: Throughout your day, pause and appreciate the simple pleasures – a warm cup of tea, a kind gesture, or a beautiful sunset.

A Gratitude Journal to Transform Your World

On my website, you'll find a powerful tool that can accompany you on this journey of gratitude – "Dear God: 365 Days of Thankfulness to Transform Your World." This journal is a companion for your daily gratitude practice, guiding you through a year of mindful appreciation. By embracing gratitude and incorporating it into your daily life, you're embarking on a journey of transformation that can lead you from burnout to a life illuminated by positivity, purpose, and a heart full of blessings.

Exploring the Role of Prayer and Spiritual Connection: Navigating the Path of the Soul

In the voyage of self-discovery and inner peace, the exploration of prayer and spiritual connection unfolds as a sacred journey that beckons you to venture within. This section delves into the essence of these practices, guiding you through the realms of prayer and unveiling the transformative impact of nurturing your spiritual connection. By understanding the significance of prayer and embracing its various levels, you'll embark on a voyage that resonates with the depth of your soul.

Understanding Prayer and Spiritual Connection: A Divine Dialogue

Prayer: At its core, prayer is a heartfelt conversation with a higher power, the universe, or the essence of your inner self. It's an opportunity to express gratitude, seek guidance, and find solace in the embrace of the divine.

Spiritual Connection: This is the ethereal thread that links you to something greater than yourself. It's a path of inner exploration, a quest to tap into the profound wisdom that resides within and beyond.

Why Exploring Prayer and Spiritual Connection Matters

In a world that often prioritizes material pursuits, exploring prayer and spiritual connection serves as an anchor to your inner sanctum. These practices remind you that there's more to life than what meets the eye, offering a sanctuary for reflection, solace, and communion with the sacred.

Nurturing Your Spiritual Essence Through Prayer

Fostering Inner Stillness: Prayer quiets the mind and creates a space for inner reflection, allowing you to connect with your spiritual essence.

Seeking Guidance: Through prayer, you open a channel to seek guidance, clarity, and answers to life's questions.

Finding Comfort: Prayer provides solace in times of turmoil, nurturing your emotional well-being and soothing your soul.

The Three Levels of Prayer: Insights from St. Teresa of Avila

First Level - Vocal Prayer: This is when you recite prayers using words, allowing them to be an expression of your heart's intention and devotion.

Second Level - Meditative Prayer: In this level, you move beyond the words and enter into deeper contemplation. You engage with the essence of the prayer, pondering its meaning and connecting with its spiritual significance.

Third Level - Contemplative Prayer: At this pinnacle, you transcend the constructs of language and thought. It's a state of silent union with the divine, where you connect on a level that goes beyond words and concepts.

Embarking on the Journey of Spiritual Connection

Create a Sacred Space: Designate a tranquil corner where you can engage in prayer and meditation without distractions.

Set Intentions: Before prayer, set your intention for connection, guidance, or simply being present.

Breath and Presence: Begin with deep, conscious breaths to ground yourself in the present moment.

Engage in Vocal Prayer: Start with vocal prayer, expressing your thoughts and feelings.

Move into Meditation: Transition to meditative prayer, allowing the words to take on deeper meaning.

Embrace Contemplation: Gradually, as you progress in your practice, experiment with contemplative prayer, sinking into the silence of your inner world.

As you traverse the path of prayer and spiritual connection, you're embarking on an odyssey of self-discovery and inner wisdom. These practices aren't confined to religious frameworks; they are pathways of the soul, journeys that transcend the boundaries of dogma. By embracing the various levels of prayer and nurturing your spiritual connection, you're embarking on a voyage that deepens your understanding of yourself, the universe, and the profound tapestry that weaves it all together.

CHAPTER 9
Creating Supportive Relationships: The Pillars of Resilience

In the tapestry of well-being, the threads of supportive relationships weave a fabric of strength and comfort. This section delves into the profound importance of creating supportive connections, shedding light on why they matter and how they play a pivotal role in your journey toward resilience. By understanding the significance of cultivating a network of support, you'll uncover a wellspring of emotional fortitude and discover the lifelines that can anchor you through life's challenges.

Why Creating Supportive Relationships Matters

Supportive relationships are the lighthouses that guide us through the storms of life. They act as a refuge where we can seek solace, share burdens, and find validation. Nurturing these connections is a cornerstone of holistic well-being.

The Crucial Importance of Supportive Relationships

Emotional Scaffolding: Supportive relationships provide a scaffold that holds you up when you're feeling vulnerable or overwhelmed.

Shared Experiences: These connections allow you to share your joys and sorrows, knowing that you're not alone on your journey.

Boosted Resilience: Supportive relationships act as a buffer against stress and adversity, enhancing your ability to bounce back from challenges.

What are Supportive Relationships?

Supportive relationships encompass a spectrum of connections that uplift, encourage, and offer a safe space for vulnerability. They can be friendships, family ties, or partnerships that foster mutual trust, empathy, and open communication.

Recognizing a Supportive Network

Empathy: Supportive individuals listen attentively and empathize with your experiences, providing a shoulder to lean on.

Non-Judgmental Attitude: A supportive network refrains from passing judgment and allows you to express yourself without fear.

Reciprocity: These relationships are built on give-and-take, where both parties contribute to the emotional well-being of the other.

Encouragement: A supportive network uplifts you, offering words of encouragement and helping you navigate challenges.

Nurturing Your Circle of Support

Express Vulnerability: Open up about your struggles and fears. Vulnerability fosters deeper connections.

Be Available: Be present for your loved ones in times of need, extending the same support you seek.

Clear Communication: Communicate your needs and boundaries clearly, ensuring a healthy dynamic.

Celebrate Success: Supportive relationships aren't just for tough times. Celebrate achievements and joys together.

Cultivating a Strong Foundation of Support

Supportive relationships are an investment in your well-being. They're the safety net that catches you when you stumble and the cheerleaders that applaud your successes. By nurturing these connections, you're cultivating a fertile ground for resilience to flourish. As you forge bonds of understanding, empathy, and care, you're fortifying yourself against life's challenges and ensuring that you're never alone on your journey toward well-being.

Building a Support Network: The Architecture of Resilience

In the blueprint of well-being, constructing a sturdy support network is akin to erecting pillars of strength that stand resolute against life's challenges. This section delves into the profound importance of building a support network, illuminating why it matters and how it's instrumental in bolstering your resilience. By understanding the significance of forging connections and seeking assistance, you'll unlock the transformative power of shared support and discover the lifelines that can uplift you in times of need.

Why Building a Support Network Matters

A support network acts as a safety net that catches you when you falter and a web of care that envelops you in times of vulnerability. The presence of such a network isn't just comforting; it's essential for your mental, emotional, and even physical well-being.

The Crucial Importance of a Support Network

Emotional Armor: A support network fortifies your emotional well-being, providing a safe haven where you can share your struggles and fears.

Collective Wisdom: With a network, you gain access to diverse perspectives and insights that can guide you through life's challenges.

Heightened Resilience: Support networks amplify your capacity to bounce back from adversity, equipping you with the strength to weather storms.

Constructing Your Support Network

Open Channels of Communication: Keep the lines of communication open with friends, family, and potential support figures. Be willing to share your thoughts and feelings.

Quality Over Quantity: Focus on cultivating a few meaningful connections rather than a multitude of superficial ones.

Nurture Mutual Support: Be available and supportive to others, fostering a reciprocal dynamic that nurtures both parties.

Stay Connected: Regularly reach out to your network, whether it's through conversations, messages, or in-person interactions.

From Isolation to Empowerment

Reflecting on my own journey, I once embraced solitude for months at a time, thinking that strength was forged in isolation. However, that path only led to the manifestation of depression and anxiety. I found myself spending months in bed, trapped in a cycle of despair.

It was only when I recognized the need for a robust support network that I began to experience transformative change. Today, I stand fortified by a network that includes family, spiritual soul sisters, adopted godmothers, a priest, counselors, coaches, and business mentors. These connections have become my pillars of strength.

Strength in Unity, Not Solitude

We're conditioned to believe that strength lies in self-sufficiency, but the truth is that seeking support doesn't signify weakness; it's a testament to your courage and self-awareness. Relying on a network is a display of strength, not fragility. It's an acknowledgment that you don't have to navigate life's challenges alone.

In Unity, There's Empowerment

With a solid support network, you're transformed from a solitary warrior into a unified force. The collective wisdom, empathy, and encouragement of your network empower you to face challenges head-on. As you lean on these connections, you'll discover that you're stronger, more resilient, and capable of thriving in the face of adversity. Remember, building a support network isn't an admission of weakness; it's a declaration of your commitment to your well-being and your determination to embrace the strength that comes from unity.

Communicating Your Needs and Seeking Help: A Path to Holistic Growth

In the realm of self-care, understanding the importance of communicating your needs and seeking help is akin to discovering a wellspring of empowerment. This section delves into the profound significance of acknowledging your emotions and voicing your needs, unraveling why this practice matters and how it's intrinsically tied to your overall well-being. By embracing the wisdom of Maslow's hierarchy of needs and exploring how seeking assistance transformed my own journey, you'll uncover the transformative power of asking for help.

Why Communicating Your Needs and Seeking Help Matters

Acknowledging your emotions and expressing your needs are fundamental acts of self-care. They act as the building blocks of self-awareness, resilience, and personal growth. By honoring your emotional landscape and seeking assistance when needed, you're nurturing the very essence of your well-being.

The Crucial Role of Emotions and Needs

Emotions: Our emotions are the compasses that guide us through life's complexities. Recognizing and understanding our emotions is the cornerstone of healthy self-expression.

Needs: Our needs are the pillars upon which our well-being rests. Addressing our needs ensures that we're equipped to navigate life's challenges and thrive.

Maslow's Hierarchy of Needs: Navigating the Ladder of Fulfillment

Physiological Needs: These are the foundational needs for survival – air, water, food, shelter, and sleep.

Safety Needs: Once basic survival is ensured, safety needs come into focus – physical security, employment, health, and well-being.

Love and Belonging: Emotional well-being takes precedence with the need for love, affection, and a sense of belonging from relationships.

Esteem Needs: Self-esteem, confidence, and respect become vital as you strive to fulfill your potential and gain recognition.

Self-Actualization: The pinnacle of the hierarchy, self-actualization is the pursuit of personal growth, realization of potential, and fulfillment of creative aspirations.

How to Seek Help and Communicate Your Needs

Recognize Signals: Tune into your emotions and recognize when you're struggling, anxious, or in need of support.

Open Up: Initiate conversations with friends, family, or professionals about your emotions and needs.

Be Specific: Clearly communicate what you need and how others can provide assistance.

Professional Help: Seek assistance from professionals, such as coaches, counselors, therapists, or mentors.

The Network of Support: Who to Seek Help From

Business Coach: For business-related challenges and growth strategies.

Weight Loss Coach: To foster a healthy relationship with your body and mind.

Counselor: For navigating grief, trauma, or emotional struggles.

Mentors and Advisors: To gain insights from those with experience.

Financial Advisors: Seek guidance from financial advisors to manage your finances, set savings goals, and plan for your future financial security.

Spiritual Healers: Connect with spiritual healers who can provide guidance, energy healing, and spiritual insights to enhance your inner well-being.

Naturopathic Doctor: Consult with naturopaths to explore holistic approaches to health, including herbal remedies, nutrition, and natural therapies.

Life Coach: Engage with a life coach to work on personal development, goal setting, and creating a fulfilling life path.

Therapists: Consider therapy from different therapeutic modalities such as cognitive-behavioral therapy, psychodynamic therapy, or art therapy to address mental health concerns.

Career Coaches: Collaborate with career coaches to explore new professional directions, improve job satisfaction, and achieve career goals.

Nutritionists: Receive guidance from nutritionists to create personalized meal plans, improve eating habits, and optimize your health.

Relationship Coaches: Engage in relationship coaching to enhance communication, resolve conflicts, and strengthen personal relationships.

Life Purpose Coach: Connect with coaches specialized in helping you discover your life purpose and align your actions with your core values.

Wellness Retreat Leaders: Attend wellness retreats led by experienced leaders to immerse yourself in transformative experiences for physical, mental, and emotional well-being.

Meditation Teachers: Learn meditation techniques from experienced meditation teachers to cultivate mindfulness and reduce stress.

Holistic Therapists: Explore holistic therapies such as acupuncture or aromatherapy to promote balance and healing.

Public Speaking Coaches: Develop effective communication skills and boost your confidence with guidance from public speaking coaches.

Motivational Speakers: Attend seminars or workshops led by motivational speakers to gain inspiration and perspective on personal growth.

Parenting Coaches: Benefit from parenting coaches who provide strategies and support for navigating the challenges of parenthood.

Financial Coaches: Collaborate with financial coaches who specialize in teaching budgeting, saving, and debt management skills.

Time Management Experts: Learn efficient time management techniques from experts to balance work, personal life, and self-care.

Health and Fitness Trainers: Enlist the help of fitness trainers who create personalized workout plans and guide you toward achieving physical wellness.

Elevating Your Overall Well-Being

Asking for help doesn't signify weakness; it's a testament to your commitment to growth. By addressing your needs and seeking assistance, you're nurturing yourself on every level – physically, emotionally, and spiritually. My journey is a testament to this truth. I sought guidance in various facets of life, addressing gaps with the expertise of those who could propel me forward.

The Ever-Evolving Journey

Life's journey is a tapestry woven from diverse experiences, and each moment brings its own needs and challenges. Seeking assistance isn't a one-time act; it's a lifelong practice. Whether it's a business challenge, a personal struggle, or a moment of introspection, know that you're never alone on this path. By embracing your emotions, voicing your needs, and seeking help, you're building a solid foundation for holistic well-being and personal growth. Remember, it's not only okay to ask for help; it's a transformative act of empowerment.

Chapter 10
The Role of Physical Health: Nurturing the Mind-Body Connection

In the intricate dance of well-being, the role of physical health takes center stage as a cornerstone of resilience and vitality. This section delves into the profound importance of nurturing the mind-body connection, drawing insights from the principles of mind-body nutrition as espoused by Marc David. By understanding why physical health matters and exploring actionable steps to foster a harmonious relationship between your mind and body, you'll unearth the transformative power of holistic wellness.

Why Physical Health is Paramount

Physical health is the bedrock upon which the tapestry of well-being is woven. It's the vessel through which we experience life, and it plays an integral role in our mental, emotional, and spiritual states. By prioritizing your physical well-being, you're creating a fertile ground for resilience to flourish.

The Mind-Body Connection: Insights from Mind-Body Nutrition

Mind-body nutrition, as championed by Marc David, underscores the intricate interplay between our thoughts, emotions, and physical health. It emphasizes the significance of nourishing not only our bodies but also our minds, nurturing a holistic approach to wellness.

The Physical-Emotional Link

Our physical health and emotional well-being are intrinsically linked. Emotions can impact our eating habits, digestion, and overall health, while our physical well-being can influence our mental state and emotional resilience.

Fostering Physical Health

Nutrition: Embrace a balanced and nourishing diet that fuels your body and supports your energy levels. Mindful eating, as advocated by Marc David, encourages conscious awareness of your body's needs and signals.

Physical Activity: Engage in regular physical activity that suits your preferences and capabilities. Exercise not only benefits your body but also enhances your mood and mental clarity.

Restful Sleep: Prioritize sleep as a foundation for overall well-being. Quality sleep supports mental clarity, emotional balance, and physical recovery.

Hydration: Drink ample water to maintain proper bodily functions, cognitive sharpness, and emotional equilibrium.

Honoring the Mind-Body Connection

By nurturing your physical health, you're tending to the very vessel that houses your thoughts, emotions, and aspirations. The principles of mind-body nutrition remind us that our relationship with food and our bodies is deeply intertwined with our mental and emotional well-being. As you prioritize balanced nutrition, physical activity, rest, and hydration, you're fostering a harmonious connection between your mind and body.

The Symphony of Wellness

Your body and mind are interconnected instruments that compose the symphony of your life. Nourishing your physical health isn't a mere chore; it's a powerful act of self-love and self-care. By embracing the teachings of mind-body nutrition and honoring the mind-body connection, you're orchestrating a melody of holistic wellness that resonates through every facet of your existence. As you tend to your physical well-being, you're not only fortifying your resilience but also nurturing the harmony that allows you to thrive.

Exercise, Nutrition, and Sleep: A Trifecta for Holistic Wellness

In the grand tapestry of well-being, the threads of exercise, nutrition, and sleep intricately weave together, forming a harmonious trinity that sustains our physical and mental health. Understanding the principles of mind-body nutrition, as elucidated by Marc David, underscores the profound impact our thoughts and emotions have on our bodily realities. Let's explore how each element contributes to our holistic wellness, while drawing from personal experiences and research to shed light on their transformative power.

Exercise: Moving Mindfully for Balance

Mind-body nutrition teaches us that our thoughts and emotions influence the outcomes of our exercise routines. If we approach exercise with dread, we may inadvertently trigger cortisol production, leading to stress and weight gain. Personal experience underscores this truth: I found myself over exercising, fueled by adrenaline and stress from dawn till dusk. The result? Burnout and a 20kg weight gain. The lesson is clear – choosing exercise that resonates with you and reduces stress is crucial.

Nutrition: Nourishing with Gratitude and Mindfulness

Drawing insights from Marc David's teachings and Marianne Williamson's wisdom, we learn that nourishing our bodies is an act of gratitude and self-care. Before eating, take a moment to slow down, breathe, and express gratitude. This mindful approach enhances digestion, optimizes nutrient absorption, and fosters a healthier relationship with food. Incorporating Marianne Williamson's lessons from "A Course in Weight Loss" empowers us to address emotional triggers and transform our thoughts about food.

Sleep: The Foundation of Restoration

Research reveals that adequate sleep is essential for different age groups. For adults aged 18-64, 7-9 hours of sleep are recommended, while older adults (65+) benefit from 7-8 hours. Sleep rejuvenates our bodies, strengthens cognitive function, and enhances emotional resilience. By prioritizing restful sleep, we're nurturing our physical, mental, and emotional well-being.

The Mind-Body Connection: Thoughts Shape Realities

Mind-body nutrition elucidates the profound connection between our thoughts and our bodily experiences. Marc David's teachings underscore that our thoughts can influence how our bodies process food, react to exercise, and even determine our weight. By adopting positive, mindful thoughts, we're creating a positive feedback loop that nurtures our overall wellness.

A Personal Transformation: Balancing Exercise

Once burdened by overexercising, I recognized the need for balance. Now, daily walks of 4-8kms have rewarded me with weight loss and renewed vitality. By listening to my body and choosing exercise that aligns with my well-being, I've reclaimed my physical health and mental equilibrium.

A Nutritional Paradigm Shift: Eating with Gratitude

Incorporating the practice of eating with gratitude has transformed my relationship with food. Taking mindful breaths and expressing thanks before meals has become a sacred ritual that enhances digestion and appreciation for nourishment.

The Gift of Restful Sleep: Prioritizing Restoration

By honoring the recommended sleep durations for my age, I've unlocked the benefits of restful sleep. I awaken refreshed, ready to face the day with mental clarity and emotional resilience.

Holistic Wellness through Mind-Body Nutrition

As we align exercise, nutrition, and sleep with the principles of mind-body nutrition, we're sculpting a path to holistic wellness. The fusion of these elements, guided by the wisdom of Marc David and the insights of personal experiences, empowers us to navigate life with vitality, joy, and a deeper understanding of the intricate interplay between our minds and bodies.

Holistic Approaches to Well-Being: Nurturing Every Facet of You

Holistic approaches to well-being embrace the entirety of your being – mind, body, spirit, and emotions – recognizing that each facet is interconnected and influences the others. This section delves into the significance of holistic well-being, unraveling why it matters and providing insights into the actions you can take to cultivate a harmonious and balanced life. By adopting a holistic perspective, you'll embark on a transformative journey that encompasses every aspect of your existence.

Understanding Holistic Approaches

Holistic approaches to well-being encompass a comprehensive view of your entire self. Rather than isolating individual components, these approaches recognize the intricate interplay between your thoughts, emotions, physical health, and spiritual connection. By addressing each dimension, you're fostering a state of harmony that radiates through your entire being.

The Significance of Holistic Well-Being

Prioritizing holistic well-being is an investment in your overall quality of life. It acknowledges that true well-being isn't just the absence of illness; it's the presence of vitality, fulfillment, and a sense of purpose. When all dimensions of your existence are nurtured, you're better equipped to navigate life's challenges and thrive in the face of adversity.

Nurturing Every Facet of You

Mind: Engage in practices that cultivate mental clarity, such as mindfulness meditation, journaling, and positive self-talk. Embrace learning, challenge negative thought patterns, and feed your mind with enriching content.

Body: Prioritize physical health through nourishing nutrition, regular exercise, and adequate rest. Listen to your body's cues, practice mindful eating, and choose movement that resonates with you.

Spirit: Foster a connection with your inner spirit through practices that resonate with your beliefs. Whether through prayer, meditation, nature walks, or reflection, cultivate a sense of purpose and connection beyond the material realm.

Emotions: Honor your emotions by acknowledging and expressing them in healthy ways. Engage in self-compassion, seek emotional support when needed, and learn to navigate your emotional landscape with mindfulness.

How to Embrace a Holistic Approach

Self-Awareness: Begin by tuning into each dimension of yourself – mind, body, spirit, and emotions. Understand your needs, desires, and areas that require nurturing.

Balance: Strive to create a balanced lifestyle that encompasses all facets. Allocate time and energy to each dimension, ensuring that none is neglected.

Integration: Recognize the interconnectedness of each dimension. For example, a calm mind can positively impact your emotional state, which in turn influences your physical health.

Personalized Approach: Understand that your holistic journey is unique. Tailor practices and approaches to your individual preferences and needs.

Embarking on Your Holistic Journey

Holistic approaches to well-being empower you to become the architect of your own life. By nurturing every facet of your being, you're fostering a state of equilibrium that enables you to navigate life with resilience, joy, and a profound sense of purpose. As you embark on this transformative journey, remember that well-being isn't a destination but a continuous, harmonious dance that nurtures your mind, body, spirit, and emotions.

Chapter 11
Sustaining Change and Preventing Relapse: The Art of Enduring Transformation

In the symphony of personal growth, sustaining change is the harmonious note that resounds long after the initial transformation. This section delves into the significance of sustaining change, highlighting its importance, benefits, and the transformative impact it has over the long term. It also explores the art of preventing relapses, a vital skill that guards against the pitfalls of reverting to old patterns. Drawing from personal experiences, we'll unveil the lessons learned from the perils of forsaking one's own needs to fit in.

Understanding Sustaining Change

Sustaining change isn't merely about initial success; it's about maintaining your transformation over the long haul. It involves integrating new habits, thought patterns, and approaches into your daily life to ensure enduring growth and well-being.

Why Sustaining Change Matters

Sustaining change is the linchpin that propels you from fleeting progress to lasting transformation. It's the difference between temporary shifts and lifelong evolution. It matters because your growth deserves to flourish in the landscape of your existence, enriching every moment and reshaping your future.

The Long-Term Benefits of Sustaining Change

Lasting Results: Sustaining change translates fleeting success into permanent progress, ensuring that your efforts yield tangible, enduring results.

Resilience: The practice of sustaining change fortifies your resilience, enabling you to weather challenges and setbacks with grace and determination.

Self-Empowerment: Consistently maintaining your transformation empowers you to take charge of your life and shape your destiny.

Preventing Relapses: Guarding Against Regression

Self-Awareness: Recognize the triggers, patterns, and situations that could potentially lead to relapse. Be attuned to the warning signs and red flags.

Strengthen Your Support System: Surround yourself with individuals who support your growth and well-being. Lean on your network during challenging times.

Self-Care: Prioritize self-care as a means of nurturing your overall well-being. Fill your cup regularly to prevent burnout and vulnerability to relapse.

Mindfulness: Practice mindfulness to stay present and attuned to your emotions. Mindfulness equips you to respond thoughtfully, rather than reacting impulsively.

Learning from Experience: The Pitfalls of Fitting In

Drawing from personal experience, I once relapsed due to the desire to fit in and neglecting my own needs. In an attempt to mold myself to others' expectations, I disregarded my own well-being. The outcome was detrimental – a temporary veneer of conformity that led to a steep emotional decline.

Embrace Your Authenticity: Meeting Your Own Needs

The lesson learned is that fitting in at the cost of self-neglect is a recipe for relapse. True growth involves honoring your authenticity and meeting your own needs. Recognize that your well-being isn't negotiable, and seeking validation from others pales in comparison to the empowerment that comes from staying true to yourself.

A Lifelong Dance of Transformation

Sustaining change isn't a singular act but an ongoing dance that intertwines with every facet of your existence. It's about weaving new habits into the fabric of your daily life, nurturing growth, and embodying transformation. By preventing relapses through self-awareness, self-care, and mindfulness, you're ensuring that your journey is one of consistent evolution, resilience, and empowerment. Remember, your commitment to enduring growth is a testament to your determination to live a life of purpose, authenticity, and unwavering self-love.

Monitoring Progress and Adjusting Strategies: Navigating the Path of Evolution

In the tapestry of personal growth, the practice of monitoring progress and adjusting strategies serves as a compass that guides your journey of transformation. This section delves into the essence of this practice, explaining why it's pivotal, how to engage in it, and the tools that can aid you in the process. By embracing the art of vigilance and adaptability, you'll pave a smoother path toward your desired outcomes.

Understanding Monitoring Progress and Adjusting Strategies

Monitoring progress entails tracking your advancements, setbacks, and shifts as you move along the path of change. Adjusting strategies involves modifying your approaches based on the insights gleaned from monitoring, ensuring that you remain aligned with your goals.

Why Monitoring Progress Matters

Monitoring progress offers a dual benefit: it provides a tangible record of your growth and allows you to pinpoint what's working and what's not. This awareness is invaluable as it empowers you to make informed decisions about the strategies you employ.

The What, Why, and How of Monitoring Progress

Habit Trackers: Employ habit trackers to monitor your daily routines and behaviors. These tools visually represent your progress, keeping you accountable and motivated.

Journaling: Document your thoughts, feelings, and experiences regularly. Journaling offers insight into your emotional landscape and the impact of your strategies on your well-being.

Data Collection: If applicable, gather data related to your goals. For instance, track your exercise duration, sleep patterns, or dietary intake.

Tools to Assist: The Power of Apps

Habit Tracker: This app allows you to track your habits, offering visual cues of your progress and areas of improvement.

Daylio: A mood and habit tracker that helps you gain insights into your emotional state and the factors influencing it.

MyFitnessPal: Perfect for tracking nutrition and exercise, this app provides data-driven insights into your health and well-being.

Adjusting Strategies: A Flexible Approach to Growth

Regular Review: Schedule regular intervals to review your progress and evaluate the effectiveness of your strategies.

Identify Patterns: Notice recurring patterns or trends in your progress. This insight can help you identify strategies that are yielding positive outcomes and those that may need adjustment.

Experimentation: Be open to trying new approaches and strategies based on your observations. Adaptability is key to staying aligned with your evolving needs.

Adapting for Success: Strategies to Modify

Time Management: If your schedule is affecting your progress, consider adjusting your time allocation to better suit your goals.

Exercise Routine: If your fitness regimen is causing strain or burnout, modify it to ensure balance and sustainability.

Nutrition Plan: Adjust your dietary approach if you're not seeing the desired outcomes. Seek professional guidance if needed.

Evolving with Vigilance and Flexibility

Monitoring progress and adjusting strategies is an art that marries mindfulness with adaptability. By keeping a watchful eye on your journey, you're empowered to refine your approach, fostering a proactive stance in your growth. Through tools like habit trackers and apps, you gain insights that guide your choices. Embracing flexibility in your strategies ensures that your path to transformation remains sustainable and aligned with your ever-changing needs. As you evolve, remember that progress is a dance of vigilance and adaptability – a harmonious rhythm that propels you toward your desired destination.

Strategies for Long-Term Burnout Prevention

Here's a list of 50 strategies for long-term burnout prevention:

Prioritize self-care as non-negotiable.

Set clear boundaries in work and personal life.

Practice mindfulness and meditation daily.

Engage in regular physical activity you enjoy.

Cultivate a nourishing sleep routine.

Embrace a balanced and mindful approach to nutrition.

Practice gratitude and journal your blessings.

Surround yourself with a supportive network.

Seek professional help when needed.

Pursue hobbies and passions that bring joy.

Practice deep breathing and relaxation techniques.

Establish a healthy work-life balance.

Say "no" when necessary without guilt.

Delegate tasks to ease your workload.

Take breaks throughout the day.

Disconnect from technology for designated periods.

Engage in creative expression.

Regularly assess and adjust your goals.

Engage in regular self-reflection.

Learn to manage stress effectively.

Practice self-compassion and self-love.

Set achievable goals to avoid overwhelm.

Embrace a clutter-free and organized environment.

Prioritize quality over quantity in tasks.

Foster positive relationships in your life.

Learn to manage your time efficiently.

Practice assertive communication.

Incorporate humor and laughter into your day.

Seek out moments of solitude and quiet.

Attend workshops and seminars for personal growth.

Practice forgiveness and release past burdens.

Invest time in hobbies that promote relaxation.

Engage in acts of kindness and volunteer work.

Reflect on your values and align with them.

Explore spiritual practices that resonate with you.

Maintain a positive inner dialogue.

Identify and challenge negative thought patterns.

Practice the art of saying "yes" to yourself.

Engage in regular social activities.

Set realistic expectations for yourself.

Practice time management techniques.

Engage in regular intellectual stimulation.

Seek out nature and fresh air.

Learn to ask for help when needed.

Foster a growth mindset.

Set short-term and long-term goals.

Limit exposure to negative influences.

Embrace minimalism to simplify life.

Learn to let go of perfectionism.

Celebrate your successes and milestones.

Conclusion

Congratulations on Your Journey of Transformation

Celebrating Your Journey: Embrace the Power of Acknowledgment

As we conclude this transformative journey, I invite you to take a moment to reflect on something that might have once been foreign to me, as it perhaps resonates with your own experience. It's the art of celebration – a practice that often eluded me as I raced through life like a bullet train, checking boxes and hurrying to the next chapter. Perhaps you can relate; the notion of stopping to celebrate seemed trivial in the grand scheme of things.

Yet, along this journey, I've unearthed a profound truth – life is meant to be celebrated. Every step, every effort, every milestone – big or small – deserves acknowledgment and applause. Celebrating is not just about throwing a party; it's about acknowledging the essence of your journey, the growth you've achieved, and the strides you've made.

For so long, I brushed past accomplishments, dismissing them as mere checkpoints on a timeline. But now, I understand the power of celebrating. It's not just about the event; it's about the energy and intention behind it. Celebration opens the floodgates of abundance. It tells the universe that you are grateful, that you honor your progress, and that you're open to receiving more.

Try it for yourself. When you accomplish a goal, no matter how seemingly insignificant, take a moment to acknowledge it. Whether it's treating yourself to your favorite dessert, writing a heartfelt journal entry, or sharing your success with loved ones, let yourself bask in the glow of your achievement.

Embrace the joy that comes with celebration, and you'll find that it's a catalyst for more positive experiences to flow into your life. Small or big, every success is worthy of a celebration. So, as you continue on your journey of well-being, remember to pause, honor your accomplishments, and celebrate the magnificent tapestry of your life. After all, life's beauty lies not just in the destination, but in every step of the journey.

Embracing a Balanced and Fulfilling Life: The Symphony of Well-Being

In the orchestra of life, achieving balance isn't merely a distant melody; it's the harmonious symphony that resonates throughout your existence. This section illuminates the significance of embracing balance and offers insights into how to integrate equilibrium into your daily routines. By doing so, you pave the way for a life that radiates fulfillment and contentment.

Understanding the Importance of Balance

Balance isn't a mere luxury; it's a necessity that fuels your well-being on multiple fronts. It ensures that you don't overextend in one area while neglecting another, cultivating a holistic sense of harmony that touches your physical, emotional, and spiritual dimensions.

Why Balance Matters

In a world often driven by extremes, embracing balance provides a refuge from the wear and tear of modern life. It shields you from the detrimental effects of burnout and the stressors that come with unmitigated busyness. A balanced life also fosters resilience, enabling you to navigate challenges with grace and poise.

Nurturing Balance in Your Life

Prioritize Self-Care: Dedicate time each day for activities that rejuvenate your mind, body, and spirit. Whether it's meditation, exercise, or leisurely reading, self-care anchors your well-being.

Set Boundaries: Define clear boundaries in work, relationships, and personal time. Establishing limits safeguards against overexertion and ensures that you have the space to recharge.

Create a Routine: Develop a daily routine that includes time for work, leisure, rest, and social connections. A structured routine fosters predictability and minimizes chaotic energy.

Practice Mindfulness: Engage in mindfulness practices that keep you rooted in the present moment. Mindfulness douses the flames of overthinking and enhances your ability to make balanced choices.

Reflect on Values: Regularly assess your values and priorities. Aligning your choices with your core values guides you toward activities that resonate deeply with your true self.

A Fulfilling Life Through Balance

Embracing balance is the compass that steers you away from the extremes and toward a fulfilling life. As you cultivate equilibrium, you unlock the potential to experience joy, contentment, and a profound sense of purpose. You'll find that by nurturing balance, your relationships flourish, your creativity soars, and your resilience deepens.

When you honor each aspect of your life and allocate time for self-care, work, relationships, and personal growth, you create a tapestry of well-being that is both vibrant and fulfilling. A balanced life allows you to savor every moment, magnifying the sweetness of your triumphs and providing solace during challenges.

In your pursuit of well-being, remember that balance isn't a one-time achievement; it's a continuous dance that evolves with your changing circumstances. By nurturing balance in your life, you empower yourself to live authentically, cultivate joy, and embrace the enchanting melody of a life well-lived.

One Last Note...

As we draw the curtains on this journey through the realms of burnout, well-being, and personal growth, it's important to pause and acknowledge your commitment to self-discovery and healing. Your dedication to reaching this point is a testament to your strength and the value you place on your own well-being.

By delving into the pages of this book, you've taken the first steps toward preventing burnout, cultivating self-care, and embracing holistic approaches to living a life of vitality and purpose. You've explored the intricacies of self-compassion, mindfulness, and the power of meaningful experiences. You've learned to set boundaries, prioritize self-love, and build a supportive network that uplifts you on this journey.

As you move forward, remember that transformation is an ongoing process. Embrace the wisdom you've gained, apply the strategies you've discovered, and continue to nurture your well-being with unwavering dedication. You are the author of your story, and your well-being is a journey that deserves your attention and care.

From the depths of my virtual pages, I want to express my gratitude for your presence on this journey. Thank you for investing in yourself, for seeking growth, and for acknowledging that you deserve a life filled with joy, balance, and purpose.

As you close this book, I encourage you to carry the lessons you've learned and the strategies you've embraced into your daily life. May your path be one of fulfillment, resilience, and the unshakable knowledge that your well-being matters. Here's to your continued growth, well-being, and the magnificent journey that lies ahead.

With heartfelt congratulations and warmest wishes,

Alicia Ann Wade xxx

About The Author

Alicia Ann Wade, better known as Dr. Gratitude, is a renowned thought leader, speaker, and author who has made a significant impact on people's lives through her work in the field of gratitude. Alicia is a multi-award-winning author, speaker, and creator of The Gratitude Method™, a unique approach to finding happiness and fulfillment through gratitude.

After losing everything in 2015 and again in 2021, Alicia made a life-changing decision to commit to 365 days of gratitude for life. This decision led her to discover the power of gratitude, which she now shares with the world through her work as a gratitude expert. Through her books, journals, programs, and clothing line, Alicia inspires and empowers people to find joy and fulfillment by practicing gratitude daily.

Alicia's work has been recognized with multiple awards, including the International Best Selling Author Award, International Life Coach of the Year Award, and Australian Small Business of the Year Award. Her collaborative books, journals, and programs have helped countless people worldwide to transform their lives and find happiness through gratitude.

As a dynamic and engaging speaker, Alicia has delivered keynote speeches and workshops at numerous conferences, seminars, and events worldwide. She has been featured on various media outlets, and has been a guest on numerous podcasts and radio shows.

Alicia's passion and dedication to helping people find happiness through gratitude have made her a sought-after thought leader in her field. Her infectious energy and positive attitude have inspired and motivated countless individuals to transform their lives and experience the beauty of gratitude. Join Alicia and her beautiful energy to experience love, joy, and gratitude every day.

www.thegratitudemethod.com

Further Book Recommendations

"Atomic Habits: An Easy & Proven Way to Build Good Habits & Break Bad Ones" by James Clear

"The Art of Happiness" by Dalai Lama and Howard Cutler

"The Power of Now: A Guide to Spiritual Enlightenment" by Eckhart Tolle

"The 5 Second Rule: Transform your Life, Work, and Confidence with Everyday Courage" by Mel Robbins

"Awaken the Giant Within: How to Take Immediate Control of Your Mental, Emotional, Physical and Financial Destiny!" by Tony Robbins

"The Power of Intention: Learning to Co-create Your World Your Way" by Wayne W. Dyer

"A Return to Love: Reflections on the Principles of A Course in Miracles" by Marianne Williamson

"The Four Agreements: A Practical Guide to Personal Freedom" by Don Miguel Ruiz

Books By Alicia Ann Wade

Be-Outstanding

Little White Book Part 1 & 2

Gratitude A Journey Of The Soul

Forgiveness Healing Of The Soul

Self-Love Loving Your Soul

Dear God, With Gratitude

Gratitude One Question A Day

Gratitude Prayer

Unveiling Destiny

Mirror Miracles

Remember Burn Bright, Not Out

www.ingramcontent.com/pod-product-compliance
Lightning Source LLC
Chambersburg PA
CBHW061314110426
42742CB00012BA/2179